Out of Balance

Out of Balance

◆

Prescriptions for Reforming the American Litigation System

Jonathan B. Wilson

iUniverse, Inc.
New York Lincoln Shanghai

Out of Balance
Prescriptions for Reforming the American Litigation System

Copyright © 2005 by Jonathan B. Wilson

iUniverse books may be ordered through booksellers or by contacting:

iUniverse
2021 Pine Lake Road, Suite 100
Lincoln, NE 68512
www.iuniverse.com
1-800-Authors (1-800-288-4677)

Visit the Author's website at www.jonathanbwilson.com.

ISBN-13: 978-0-595-34717-9 (pbk)
ISBN-13: 978-0-595-79460-7 (ebk)
ISBN-10: 0-595-34717-7 (pbk)
ISBN-10: 0-595-79460-2 (ebk)

Printed in the United States of America

For Victoria

Contents

Acknowledgements

I'd like to thank everyone who played a role in helping and encouraging me to write this book, beginning with Joe Wargo, Mike French and Mike Kabat of Wargo & French LLP (www.wargofrench.com). Joe, Mike, Mike and all of their colleagues at Wargo & French were extremely helpful, contributing ideas and assisting with several rounds of proofreading. While all of the errors are ultimately my own, I think there are fewer of them because of the help I got from W&F. Joe and Mike have built themselves a first-rate litigation team and when I've got a case that's headed to the courtroom I sleep better at night knowing they're on my side.

I'd also like to thank Christen Carey (www.christencarey.com) for her helpful thoughts on writing and the publishing process, Guy Powell (www.demandg.com) for his thoughts on publishing and marketing, Michael Neumeier, (www.gaughanandswann.com) for his comments and referrals, and Allen Shulman, Robin Shetler, Davina Furnish and my other colleagues at Interland (www.interland.com) for their help and support.

Introduction

Dee Arnett wanted to attract more customers to his chain of Atlanta-area car wash stations and was happily surprised when a sales rep from Sunbelt Communications contacted him with an ingenious way to reach potential customers. The sales rep told Mr. Arnett that his company had a database of customers who had agreed to receive solicitations by fax and that for a relatively modest fee ($700 for 10,000 faxes), Carnett's Car Wash could reach thousands of potential customers. Mr. Arnett agreed to give it a try and paid for 73,500 faxes to go out.

Michelle Hammond claimed to have received one of the faxes. She didn't receive any other faxes that day, and had no idea the cost of paper or toner that may have been consumed by the Carnett fax, but she contacted an attorney to sue Mr. Arnett's business. The attorney introduced Ms. Hammond to the Telephone Consumer Protection Act, a 1991 federal statute that permits a person who receives a commercial fax to sue the sender for $500 (or $1,500 if the sender was "willful"). To maximize her potential recovery, Ms. Hammond styled the lawsuit as a class action on behalf of anyone else who might have received a fax from Carnett's Car Wash.

Mr. Arnett's decision to hire Sunbelt Communications was a fateful one, for while the trial court refused to allow Ms. Hammond's lawsuit to go forward as a class action, the Georgia Court of Appeals disagreed, greenlighting a lawsuit that could impose more than $110 million in damages on Carnett's Car Wash, bankrupting the company several times over.[1]

The Carnett's Car Wash case is just one example of a litigation system that nearly everyone agrees is broken. Headlines constantly repeat stories of out of control litigation, ridiculous jury verdicts, skyrocketing insurance costs and the impact of these rising costs on health care and insurance. Politicians from both

---

1. See *Hammond v. Carnett's Inc.*, 2003 WL 22319072 (Ga. State Ct. 2003) (denying class certification) and *Hammond v. Carnett's Inc.*, 266 Ga. App. 242, 596 S.E.2d 729 (2004) (reversing the trial court). The Georgia Supreme Court has granted Carnett's request to review the case. The outcome is not known at the time of this writing.

sides of the aisle agree that something is wrong and yet there is no clear, consistent rationale for what is wrong or how to fix it.

One of the reasons why the reform debate has been so disjointed is that policy-makers and journalists have spoken about the topic from anecdotal evidence. A jury somewhere will dispense an outrageous verdict in a silly case and a handful of politicians will decry the outcome. A newspaper article will report that certain kinds of healthcare are no longer available in a particular county because litigation has forced the cost of malpractice insurance to levels that make the practice of medicine no longer worthwhile. In response, a handful of politicians will propose legislative changes aimed at the symptoms they've observed: outrageous jury awards and rising insurance costs. Business, healthcare and insurance groups will support the legislation and consumer activists and trial lawyers will oppose it. The opponents of reform will bring their own anecdotes, describing outrageous injuries done to poor, defenseless consumers and accusing "big business" of taking away the rights of injured consumers.

While these attention-getting examples can be helpful in generating the public's interest in reform, they don't tell the whole story of how litigation works, how expensive litigation is, and how the expense of litigation creates costs for business that in turn affect consumers. By avoiding the root cause of litigation and its fundamental economic impacts, these anecdotes don't help the public really understand what is at stake. This book is an attempt to describe the root cause of the problem in a way that will offer policy-makers and the public a coherent view of what the problem is and how to fix it.

Before I tell you what this book is about, let me also tell you what it is not. This book is not an attempt to vilify all litigation or defend a particular industry from attack. On the contrary, litigation (when it takes place in a well-structured system) may be an appropriate way for parties to resolve disputes. Even reasonable parties will sometime disagree. Litigation is, and should be, an appropriate forum to resolve disagreements. We cannot reform the litigation process by eliminating all litigation.

This book is also not a defense of big corporations, doctors, hospitals, insurers or any other industry for that matter. Although I am employed as the general counsel of a publicly traded company, I am not using this book as a tool to condemn all plaintiffs. My company is sometimes a defendant in litigation and it is also sometimes the plaintiff. My concern is not with protecting any particular class of litigants or defending any particular industry. My view is that the current system simply does not work. It doesn't work for plaintiffs and it doesn't work for defendants. To be effective, any solution must be truly neutral and simply restore what ought to be (and in the distant past was) the rightful balance between the rights of the party initiating a lawsuit and the rights of the party defending itself.

I recognize that many plaintiffs' lawyers may take exception to this book and may suggest that I am, somehow, a tool of "big business".[2] It is an unfortunate fact that in the debate over litigation reform there has been far too much name-calling on both sides. In fact, a measure of the effectiveness of my proposals will be the volume with which the opponents of reform try to shout them down. If litigation reform is to be effective, it should reduce by a substantial fraction both the number of cases filed and the size of the claims in those cases. Consequently, if I am truly onto a possible solution here, my opponents will endorse the effectiveness of my position by the vehemence of their protest.

This book will not outline years of research or reams of economic data to justify its conclusions. There have been studies that have tried to estimate the number of cases that would be avoided if one proposal or another were adopted. With all due respect to the authors of those studies (who no doubt were trying to advance available scholarship with their efforts) I am rather skeptical of any argument that purports to predict how a human system will respond to any change in circumstances with any degree of precision. Thousands of economists, employed by hundreds of consulting firms and investment houses every month try to predict how the stock market and other economic indicators will respond to current events. They're nearly all wrong, month after month and year after year. They gauge their success by how close they came to the right answer, when the right answer is measured in fractions of a percent.

Fundamentally, any human system—whether it's the litigation system, a market system or any other system that involves the interactions of human beings—operates under a cloud of uncertainty. Human beings are inherently uncertain creatures. They may respond by greater and lesser degrees in vaguely predictable ways, but trying to predict the outcome of a human system with mathematical certitude is like trying to build a sand castle in a windstorm. You may be able to make out basic shapes and the relative location of things, but the action of the wind on the sand will make any attention to detail a wasted effort.

I have seen first hand how litigation arises, how it is managed and how it gets resolved. Because I have taken part in decisions to sue and not sue, to settle and not settle, I know what factors played a role in those decisions and how those

---

2.   By "plaintiffs' lawyers" I refer to lawyers who make a living litigating cases on behalf of plaintiffs, often on a contingent fee basis.

decisions would have changed if the rules of litigation were different. While my experience may not be representative of every litigant's, it certainly is not out of the mainstream. That experience guides much of the analysis in this book and I have tried to provide enough examples so that you will see how my experience is typical of most decision-makers involved in handling lawsuits.

Those readers with a background in the law will note that I have tried to avoid legal jargon in this book and have provided a glossary of the legal terms I wasn't able to avoid at the end. Because lawyers are taught to pay attention to details, some legal readers may note that some of the terms in the glossary are oversimplified and fail to capture nuances that may be important. That is true. The glossary provides the non-legal reader with a quick reference for basic legal terms. It is not complete and often skips over exceptions to general rules and legal concepts that may be important to lawyers but are not necessary for the lay reader to understand the arguments in this book.

I have written this book for those who like reading about the law, politics and economics even if they are not lawyers, politicians or economists. As a result, in some places I may have summarized some legal concepts to a degree that lawyers find overly-simplified. For that I do apologize. I tried to balance carefully the need for precision and detail with the goal of presenting the case for reform to as wide an audience as possible. In that effort I may have erred to one side or the other at times. In particular, attorneys may find it helpful to skip Chapter 2. That chapter is essentially a summary of what you learned in your first year civil procedure class in law school.

Another disclaimer: The ideas in this book are my own. Although my ideas are based largely on my experiences as an attorney at several large firms and as the general counsel of two companies (one private and one public) my opinions are not necessarily shared by my employers or clients, past, present or future. While I hope that this book will convince everyone of the need to change the way lawsuits are conducted in America, not everyone will share this view. Their disagreement should be with me and not with my employers or clients.

In short, I hope to convince you that the problem with the U.S. litigation system today is that it creates economic incentives for certain kinds of lawsuits. Those incentives allow plaintiffs to play the odds in a game without consequences, forcing defendants to bear exorbitant costs. Because defendants typically lack the legal right to recover their costs and attorneys' fees from the plaintiffs, many defendants settle claims based upon their reckoning of what it would cost to fight the suit and win. Knowing that many defendants will settle simply to avoid the cost of litigation, there is a sizeable industry of plaintiffs' lawyers who pursue claims of little or no merit simply in the hopes of extorting a settlement from the defendant. They can do this because the system holds few disincentives for the plaintiffs or their lawyers. The system imposes the preponderance of its costs on the defendant. It is this imbalance that generates billions of dollars in wasted costs every year.

1

The Cost of Litigation in America

To make our economy stronger and more competitive, America must reward, not punish, the efforts and dreams of entrepreneurs. Small business is the path of advancement, especially for women and minorities, so we must free small businesses from needless regulation and protect honest job-creators from junk lawsuits. Justice is distorted, and our economy is held back, by irresponsible class actions and frivolous asbestos claims. President George W. Bush, State of the Union Address, February 2, 2005.

Litigation Viewed from the Headlines

During the 2004 Presidential election both candidates agreed on the need for litigation reform. President Bush stressed the problems with medical malpractice litigation and its impact on provider insurance and the cost of health care. He backed limits on malpractice damage awards as a means of limiting that kind of litigation. Senator John Kerry, the democratic nominee, agreed that the litigation system needed reform but emphasized themes of "fairness." Even so, the Kerry campaign supported limiting attorneys' fees in medical malpractice cases, requiring advance medical certification of malpractice claims and "holding attorneys responsible" for filing frivolous claims.[3] For a campaign that was noted for its contrast between the candidates on fundamental issues, there was a fair amount of agreement that our current litigation system permits too many lawsuits to go forward and needs to be fixed. But what really is wrong with the system?

The Cost of Litigation—A Macroeconomic View

As the Congressional Budget Office notes in its 2003 report, *The Economics of U.S. Tort Liability: A Primer*, collecting comprehensive data about the U.S. litigation system is complicated by the decentralized nature of the court system, the lack of any central reporting mechanism, variations in how different state courts treat different kinds of claims and the lack of data over the private resolution of litigation.[4] As we'll discuss later in Chapter 2, under the American system of federalism, state courts handle most civil litigation with federal courts handling a smaller percentage. In addition, about one quarter of the states have unified court systems in which all cases are handled by the same court system with the other three quarters having multi-tiered court systems with separate courts for different kinds of cases (i.e., probate, small claims, etc.)

Nevertheless, the best data available suggests that there were approximately 16 million civil cases filed in 2002.[5] Civil cases are lawsuits between individual parties, usually involving a claim for money damages. In contrast, a criminal case is a prosecution by the government against an individual concerning a criminal offense. Criminal cases generally involve the government's attempt to convict a defendant and have penalties ranging from fines to imprisonment. This book only discusses civil and not criminal litigation.

Of the 16 million civil cases filed each year, approximately 40% were general civil cases while the remaining 60% were specialized cases, including small claims, estate, mental health and other kinds of cases. Small claims, estate, mental health and the other specialized cases that make up 60% of the 16 million cases are numerous but relatively inexpensive and not a significant contributor to the overall cost of litigation. Within the general civil litigation docket (40% of 16 million), the caseload was almost evenly split between tort claims and contract claims for most of the 1990s although the data for 2000-2002 shows a slight

---

3.   Statement of Senator John Edwards, October 5, 2004, *available at* http://
     www.issues2000.org/News_Tort_Reform.htm ("We do have too many lawsuits.
     And the reality is there's something that we can do about it. We want to put more
     responsibility on the lawyers to require to have the case reviewed by independent
     experts to determine if the case is serious and meritorious before it can be filed; hold
     the lawyers responsible for that, certify that and hold the lawyer financially responsi-
     ble if they don't do it; have a three-strikes-and-you're-out rule so that a lawyer who
     files three of these cases without meeting this requirement loses their right to file
     these cases. That way we keep the cases out of the system that don't belong in the
     system.")

4.   Congressional Budget Office, *The Economics of U.S. Tort Liability: A Primer* (Octo-
     ber 2003).

5.   National Center for State Courts, *Examining the Work of State Courts 2003*, available
     at http://www.ncsonline.org/C-Research/csp/CSP_Main_Page.html. This study
     defines "civil" cases as anything that is other than a criminal case.

increase in the number of contract cases in contrast to the number of tort cases. Thus, in very round terms, there are approximately 3 million tort cases and 3 million contract cases filed in state courts annually.

The economic impact of civil litigation on the U.S. economy as a whole is enormous. Unfortunately, the bulk of the data concerns only tort cases. Tort cases are those that relate to claims for compensation for injuries that are recognized by the law. Examples of torts include negligence, product liability, wrongful death and the like. In contrast, contracts cases involve disputes between parties who had some kind of agreement or contract. Chapter 2 describes the difference between these kinds of cases in more detail.

According to the leading actuarial study, the total cost of tort litigation in the U.S. in 2002 was $233 billion.[6] Of this $233 billion, approximately 22% went to compensate plaintiffs for their economic losses, 24% went to compensate plaintiffs for their noneconomic losses, 21% went to administration, 19% went to pay the attorneys fees of claimants and 14% went to pay the attorneys' fees and costs of defendants.

Components of Tort System Costs (Figure 1.1)
(All figures in billions)

1. Awards for economic loss	$51.260	22%
2. Awards for noneconomic loss	$55.920	24%
3. Administration	$48.930	21%
4. Claimants' attorney fees	$44.270	19%
5. Defense attorneys fees and costs	$32.620	14%
TOTAL	$233.000	100%

These numbers deserve some explanation. Economic loss measures the damages claimed by the plaintiff that represent the economic impact of the alleged wrong. For example, in a medical malpractice case the claimant's economic damages might include his medical expenses, lost wages or diminished capacity to earn wages flowing from the injuries caused by the malpractice. These kinds of economic damages are also called "compensatory" damages because their purpose

---

6. Tillinghast-Towers Perrin, *U.S. Tort Costs: 2003 Update.* It is noteworthy, however, that the Tillighast-Towers Perrin study characterizes tort cases slightly differently than the NCSC data, tending to understate the financial impact.

is to compensate the plaintiff for actual economic loss from the injury at issue in the case.

In contrast, noneconomic damages are those that are not tied to any actual economic harm suffered by the claimant. Noneconomic damages include both pain and suffering damages and punitive damages. While an injured plaintiff's pain and suffering may be very real, the plaintiff has not actually lost money as a result. In addition the purpose of punitive damages, as we'll discuss in more detail later, is to punish the defendant and to create incentives for the rest of society to avoid the kind of wrongdoing done by the defendant in the case. Punitive damages should act as a deterrent to future wrongdoing. Punitive damages may be a powerful incentive for a plaintiff to prosecute certain kinds of tort cases, but the punitive damages are not supposed to be a form of compensation. Compensatory, or economic damages, compensate a plaintiff for its injuries. Punitive damages are a windfall.

Although there is no comparable data available for the approximate 3 million contract cases filed annually, with some educated guesswork we can approach a ballpark number. First, as a general rule, punitive and other noneconomic damages are not available as a remedy in a breach of contract claim. On the other hand, plaintiffs in a business case involving a disputed contract often allege fraud (for which punitive damages can be available) in an attempt to get around the economic damages limitations in a breach of contract case. While I can't quantify it, at least some portion of the contracts caseload probably includes mixed claims of contract and fraud, suggesting that there would be at least some noneconomic damages in a calculation of contract case costs.

For example, in a case between two businesses in which one (a manufacturer, for example) contracted with the other (a supplier of component parts) to provide a supply of components for the manufacturer's use in building its products there might be a written contract that describes the components, their process and how the supplier is to deliver them. Let's imagine that the manufacturer discontinues selling the product that relies upon the supplier's components and let's assume that the contract contained no promises about the number of components the manufacturer would require or any profits that the supplier could expect to earn.

The supplier might sue the manufacturer for breach of the contract, but this would be a losing effort. After all, the contract makes no promise about how long the manufacturer will continue to make the product or how many units it will need to purchase from the supplier. To try to recover its investment in the components, however, the supplier might try to allege that the manufacturer engaged in fraud by making oral promises that the work would go one for years and that the supplier would be profitable, etc. In such a situation, the case would involve contractual matters and might even include a claim for breach of contract but the parties' efforts would be focused on the tort claim of fraud, with its potential for a greater damages award and even the prospect of punitive damages. Cases like this are quite common in the realm of business litigation. How a case like this would be reported in the statistics is hard to say and introduces some level of estimation into the results.

While it's hard to make any generalizations about the size of economic damages in contract cases, there is no reason to believe that the attorneys' fees and costs (both on the defense side and the plaintiff's side) should be very different from those in the tort context. A contracts case can be just as difficult to litigate as a tort case and sometimes even more so when the contract case can involve large volumes of documents or accounting evidence. Even if the cost of the U.S. contracts caseload were half of the tort caseload (with the noneconomic damages for contracts cases amounting to only 10% of the same amount for torts cases), the total annual cost would be approximately $97 billion.

Projected Cost of Contracts Cases (Figure 1.2)
(All figures in billions)

1. Awards for economic loss	$25.630	26%
2. Awards for noneconomic loss	$5.592	6%
3. Administration	$27.960	29%
4. Claimants' attorney fees	$22.135	23%
5. Defense attorneys' fees and costs	$16.310	17%
TOTAL	$97.627	100%

Adding the actual 2002 cost of tort cases (from Figure 1.1) with the projected cost of contract cases (from Figure 1.2) yields a total cost for all civil litigation in the range of $330 billion, breaking down as follows:

Cost of Civil Litigation (Figure 1.3)
(All figures in billions)

1. Awards for economic loss	$76.890	23%
2. Awards for noneconomic loss	$61.512	19%
3. Administration	$76.890	23%
4. Claimants' attorney fees	$66.405	20%
5. Defense attorneys' fees and costs	$48.930	15%
Subtotal: Transaction Costs (Items 3, 4 and 5)	$192.225	58%
TOTAL	$330.627	100%

From this point of view, it is easier to see how litigation affects the U.S. economy as a whole. Looking only at the costs of tort litigation (and excluding any estimate for contracts cases), Tillinghast-Towers Perrin estimates that, as a percentage of the U.S. gross domestic product (or GDP), tort costs amounted to 2.23% in 2002 and were expected to continue to rise to 2.45% in 2005. Historically, as a percentage of GDP, tort costs have risen fairly consistently from less that 1% in 1950, to 2% in 1980 to numbers above 2% in the 1990s and early 2000s.[7] Perhaps not surprisingly, in its 2002 study the research firm concluded that the U.S. tort system, as a percentage of GDP, was the most expensive among the twelve industrialized countries that it examined.[8] When tort costs are compared to population they amount to slightly more than $800 for every person in the U.S. If tort costs rise as predicted, that amount will surpass $1,000 per person in 2005.

"Alright," you might say, "tort litigation costs $233 billion per year and contracts litigation costs in the range of $97 billion per year and those costs, spread out over about 6 million cases per year, is somewhere in the range of $1,000 for every person in the U.S. Is this really a problem? Is there some other way for liti-

---

7. Tillinghast-Towers Perrin, *supra* n6 at 22, Appendix IA. Although there was a slight dip in tort costs as a percentage of GDP from 1997 to 2000, the Tillinghast-Towers Perrin study explains that this brief period of anomaly was the result of a surge in economic output without a corresponding surge in tort costs. *Id.* at 2.

8. Congressional Budget Office, *The Economics of U.S. Tort Liability: A Primer, supra* n4 at 20. The next two closest countries were Italy (with tort costs of 1.7% of GDP) and Germany (with tort costs of 1.3% of GDP).

gation to be more efficient? After all, there will always be disputes and they've got to be resolved somehow."

The answer is that these costs are a problem on several levels. First, as we've seen, the U.S. system is more expensive than the litigation system of any other industrialized country. Second, the costs that are spent on litigation must necessarily be diverted from other sources. Maintaining a litigation system that permits some participants to make money but that imposes most of its expense on another group entails a series of choices. Those choices have implications of their own. Finally, the macroeconomic impact of the cost of litigation represents the sum of the experiences of the participants in the U.S. economy. The $1,000 per person annual cost of excess litigation is not actually billed to each person. It is borne by certain groups of persons, thereby creating incentives that have their own impacts on the economy and on society. Legislators are responsible for the litigation system they choose through the statutes they enact. In other words, choosing to do nothing and leaving the litigation system alone entails the choice to impose most of the costs of that system on those parties who most often appear as the defendants in the system. Choosing to balance the cost of the system on one kind of party creates incentives—for both plaintiffs and defendants—that affect the economy and our society.

Balancing Efficiency and Equity

If the U.S. litigation system is broken because it is too expensive, that suggests that there is some alternative that is less expensive or that achieves some optimal level of expense that is appropriate. What would a well-balanced litigation system look like?

A well-functioning litigation system should serve two competing interests—equity and efficiency—in a way that serves equity with minimal loss of efficiency. In any particular dispute one party believes that it has been wronged by the other and seeks recompense from the defendant. The rules of right and wrong—the law—set the standards by which conduct is judged and also establish the rules through which wrongful conduct is punished and damaged victims are compensated for their losses. In a perfect system, damaged victims would recover all of their damages according to the law. In theory this would represent perfect "equity" because there would be no damage suffered by a victim that was not compensated 100% by the party who did the damage.

At the same time, in a perfect system, the process by which wrongs were judged would have the least possible cost. A system that awarded damages to

injured parties but required parties to spend enormous sums to reach a final outcome would be less efficient than a system that was cheaper or faster. Every dollar
spent on the system itself (through administrative costs and the parties' attorneys'
fees) is essentially a drain on the economy. Administrative and transaction costs
play no role in the equity of the system. They only serve to make it more expensive. Whether that expense is justified depends upon whether there is a less
expensive method of delivering the same amount of equity. If it were possible to
arrive at exactly the same results in terms of compensating parties for their injuries (and thereby achieving equity) for less, the less expensive method would be
better than a more expensive alternative. Balancing efficiency with equity, then,
should be at the heart of the matter for policy-makers. A system that was both
cheap and fast might make mistakes, leading to inequity. A system that was dili-
gent to a fault, investigating every nuance of every potential claim might result in
substantial equity but be so slow and expensive that its inefficiency drowned the
equitable results it sought to achieve. The political and policy-making exercise of
balancing efficiency with equity is at the heart of the debate on litigation reform.

In the words of the Congressional Budget Office:

> Different observers describe tort liability as serving various combinations of
> purposes—among them, compensation, deterrence, risk spreading, and pun-
> ishment or retribution. In economic terms, those various purposes can be
> related to the overarching social goals of efficiency and equity. The efficiency
> goal is to allocate scarce resources so as to maximize the total benefits available
> to society; the equity goal is to distribute those benefits in accord with some
> (necessarily subjective) conception of fairness or justice. Metaphorically speak-
> ing, efficiency involves making the pie as big as possible, and equity focuses on
> slicing it appropriately.[9]

A corollary to this maxim is that, for every dollar of inefficiency in the litigation
system there is one less dollar available for the overall benefit of society.

But how can we measure efficiency in the U.S. litigation system? We can measure efficiency both in nominal terms—what percentage of the total cost was
devoted to expenses other than victim compensation—and in comparative
terms—how the percentage of non-compensation costs compares to other systems of compensation. On both levels the U.S. litigation system leaves much to
be desired.

---

9.   *Id.* at 11.

Inefficiency in Nominal Terms

Of the $233 billion figure for the cost of tort litigation in 2002[10] only 46% ($107 billion) represented awards to claimants, with the balance (54% or $126 billion) representing administrative costs, claimants' fees and costs and defense fees and costs. Assuming that the economic awards and noneconomic awards paid to claimants are an adequate approximation of the "true" equity those claimants should have received, the current litigation system is only 46% efficient. In an ideal system, those claimants would have recovered their economic and noneconomic awards, but without the $126 billion in costs actually incurred. In other words, more than half of the entire cost of tort litigation derives from the system itself and the parties who make a living on the system. Less than half represents the actual value of compensation that the system delivers from tortfeasors (the parties who commit torts) to claimants. The system drains $126 billion out of the economy every year.

This analysis, however, tends to *overstate* the efficiency of the system. Of the $107 billion awarded to claimants, slightly less than half of that amount ($51 billion) represented economic damages. Slightly more than half ($56 billion) represented noneconomic damages. As the Tillinghast-Towers Perrin study concludes, "if viewed as a method of compensating victims for their economic losses, the tort system is extremely inefficient, returning only 22 cents of the tort cost dollar for that purpose."[11] Some commentators suggest that the tort system should be concerned primarily with economic damages and not with noneconomic (or "nonpecuniary") damages. As we will see later in this book, most of the arguments for litigation reform that involve caps on damages awards spring from the argument that the tort system should discount or limit noneconomic damages. If so, the system is indeed horribly inefficient. Even giving the benefit of the doubt to the status quo, however, an efficiency percentage of 46% must be less than optimal.

Efficiency in Comparative Terms

But what level of efficiency would be optimal? As the Council of Economic Advisors remarked when it examined the efficiency of tort litigation, "some level of

---

10. Again, this number only accounts for tort litigation and does not include the impact of contracts litigation.
11. Tillinghast-Towers Perrin, *supra* n6 at 17 (2003).

'transactions costs' is required in order to administer any system."[12] Is 56% too high?

One means of measuring comparative inefficiency is to compare the transaction costs of litigation (measured as a percentage of the economic compensation awarded to claimants) with the transaction costs of other systems of compensating victims. In its study the Council of Economic Advisors compared tort litigation to workers compensation.

The U.S. workers compensation system is a "no-fault" system of compensation. Under the law, developed in the early 20th century, all employers are required to pay into a central, state-administered fund. Workers who are injured on the job can apply to the state workers compensation fund for payment of their medical expenses. Workers who are hurt and unable to work for an extended period of time can receive from the fund the wages they would have earned had they not been disabled. Employers pay into the fund based upon their loss experience, derived primarily from the risks inherent in their businesses. Employers involved in heavy industry or dangerous occupations pay more than those primarily involved in clerical and office work. In exchange for their payments into the compensation fund, employers are immune from suit for virtually all workplace injuries suffered by their employees.

Employees also benefit from the system by having ready access to compensation for their injuries without the need to endure a lengthy litigation process. In addition, because employees are entitled to compensation regardless of their own fault in the circumstances of their injury (and without any need to prove that their employers were at fault) the system is relatively easy to administer, having no need to investigate thoroughly the facts of the case to determine the relative responsibilities of the parties.

With workers compensation as a comparator, the Council of Economic Advisors concluded that, for every dollar paid to workers compensation claimants, 23 cents were consumed in transaction costs.[13] Applying 23% as a proxy for an efficient system, the Council of Economic Advisors concluded that, if both economic and noneconomic awards are the proper measure of compensation, the tort system should deliver those awards ($107 billion in 2002) with transaction

---

12. Council of Economic Advisers, *Who Pays for Tort Liability Claims? An Economic Analysis of the U.S. Tort Liability System* (April 2002). Note that this study uses data from the 2002 Tillinghast-Towers Perrin study and not the more recent 2003 data cited elsewhere in this book. Consequently, some of the data in the CEA paper tend to understate the cost of tort litigation.

13. *Id.* at. 10.

costs equal to 23% of that amount (approximately $25 billion). Following that logic, an efficient tort system would have a transaction cost of $132 billion, instead of $233 billion, resulting in an inefficiency (or "excessive cost") of $101 billion.[14] If the value of noneconomic awards is added to the inefficiency of the system, the excessive costs rise to $158 billion.

Of course, this kind of comparison is only a "straw man". It would never be possible to replace the entire tort litigation system with a "no fault" insurance system like that of the workers compensation system. Doing so would require that funds be raised from somewhere (either directly in taxes or indirectly through contributions from market participants) and would have various incentives for inefficiency. If a universal insurance fund existed through which any potential tort plaintiff could receive compensation for its economic damages, there would be no incentive for plaintiffs to think realistically about their losses. We would all simply hold our hands out to the universal fund for compensation.

Nevertheless, as a means of thinking about the prospects of a more efficient system it is helpful to know that at least one alternative offers the chance for 23% inefficiency as opposed to the 56% inefficiency litigation offers today.

The Inefficiency of Deadweight Loss

Even inefficiency of 56%, however, tends to *understate* the inefficiency of the tort system because it accounts only for the direct costs of tort litigation and ignores the indirect costs. Those indirect costs (which economists call a "deadweight loss") arise from distortions in economic consumption and production that take place as the result of marketplace participants making choices in order to avoid litigation.[15]

Defensive medicine is just one example. Some doctors have described the phenomenon of physicians prescribing excessive or unneeded medical tests in order to avoid any possible risk of a missed diagnosis. Ninety-four percent of doctors say that unnecessary care or procedures are sometimes ordered for patients out of a fear of litigation and 91% of doctors say they have observed other doctors doing this.[16] These excessive or unneeded tests have a cost (which must be borne by a

---

14. Using 2001 data, the Council of Economic Advisors concluded that the excessive tort costs were $87 billion. By using the same logic with the benefit of 2002 data, the excessive tort costs are an additional $14 billion.

15. *Id.* at 11–12.

16. Common Good, *Law and Health Care: Polling Data Fact Sheet* (August 1, 2004), *available a*t http://cgood.org/learn-reading-cgpubs-factsheets-9.html.

combination of the physician, the patient and an insurer) but that cost is not captured in the $233 billion direct cost of tort litigation.

Deadweight loss is a difficult concept to describe because ordinary people never put a price tag on it. Congress has no line item in the federal budget for the cost of deadweight loss, and yet it exists. No one ever gets a bill in the mail for deadweight loss. And yet, perhaps even more than the direct costs of excessive litigation, deadweight loss affects everyone everyday in the form of opportunities that no longer exist because they have been forced out of existence, or rendered prohibitively expensive, as a result of the direct costs of litigation.

Some advocates of litigation reform have described the social cost of litigation like a "tax" and in one sense this is very accurate. A car manufacturer's anticipated costs of litigation get added to the price of every car that rolls off the assembly line. When you buy the car, you pay a portion of the litigation tax. The municipality that anticipates lawsuits arising from accidents that occur in its parks and playgrounds puts the cost of that litigation into its annual budget and that expense contributes to property and payroll tax bills. You pay that tax. Alternatively, if the municipality wants to avoid raising taxes, it may dismantle its playgrounds or close its parks. If so, you lose the value of having those playgrounds or parks for your use. Either way, you lose something.

The airline that anticipates getting sued considers that expense when its sets the price of a ticket. You pay that tax. If it fears getting sued by passengers who are allergic to peanuts, maybe the airline stops serving peanuts. Maybe it stops serving snacks altogether. You pay, either through a more expensive ticket or through the lost amenity. These are all examples of the deadweight loss caused by the litigation tax.

The deadweight loss is never really paid but instead is measured in terms of opportunities that no longer exist because they have been forced out of the marketplace by the litigation tax. Peter Huber described it best when he wrote:

> "Because of the tax, you cannot use a sled in Denver city parks or a diving board in New York City Schools. You cannot buy an American Motors "CJ" Jeep or a set of construction plans for novel airplanes from Burt Rutan, the pioneering designer of the *Voyager*. You can no longer buy many American-made brands of sporting goods, especially equipment for amateur contact sports such as hockey and lacrosse. For a while, you could not use public transportation in the city of St. Joseph, Missouri, nor could you go to jail in Lafayette County in the same state. Miami canceled plans for an experimental railbus because of the tax. The tax has curtailed Little League and fireworks displays, evening concerts, sailboard races, and the use of public beaches and

ice-skating rinks. It temporarily shut down the famed Cyclone at the Astro-land amusement park on Coney Island."[17]

Deadweight loss is also present in the choices that both producers and consumers make about which products to produce and consume:

- Auto manufacturers who design heavier cars for the purpose of limiting safety-related lawsuits, but which consume more fuel and are more expensive to manufacture and purchase.

- The delay in bringing new medicines to market brought about by excessive testing to avoid possible tort liability and the lives lost because those new medicines were not available when needed.

- The increase in cost of other products and services occasioned by over-engineering for safety.

- The loss of other products and services that are never developed or brought to market (or which are removed from the market) in response to the perceived cost of litigation.

I saw an example of deadweight loss just a few days ago when buying an over the counter pain reliever for our infant baby. The pain reliever is available in two varieties: an "infant formula" (ages 6 months to two years) with 50 mg of pain reliever per dose and a "young child formula" (ages 2 to 4 years) with 100 mg of pain reliever per dose. Both varieties come in the same sized bottle and both varieties cost the exact same amount. And yet, if the labeling is to be believed (and it is, because that would be another lawsuit if it weren't true) the infant formula contains precisely half of the pain reliever of the young child formula. Why are both bottles priced the same? Why are there two "formulas"? Why not simply sell the "young child formula" but tell the parents of infants under two years of ago to use only a half dose? I'm sure that somewhere there was an in-house attorney at the pharmaceutical company who had the task of considering the higher likelihood of product liability claims from the infant formula as opposed to the young child formula. That increased chance of liability and the cost associated with that litigation, essentially accounts for the redundant product line and its (effectively) doubled price.

---

17. Peter W. Huber, LIABILITY: THE LEGAL REVOLUTION AND ITS CONSEQUENCES (1988) at 4.

Measuring deadweight loss, by definition, is necessarily a matter of guesswork: you cannot measure the value of things that didn't happen (or that happened later or that become more expensive than should have been the case). On the other hand, the concept of deadweight loss is a very real phenomenon and not the product of an economist's imagination. As the Council of Economic Advisors concluded "Anecdotal evidence suggests that some products that may have a net benefit to society as a whole are withheld from the marketplace due to excessive concerns of liability from the tort system."[18] The measure of deadweight loss, however, is "the difference between the value of the good that is not produced and the value of the next best alternative. Because only one of these goods is produced in the market, it is difficult to assess this loss." The Council of Economic Advisors, citing the analysis of a Harvard University professor, suggested that the deadweight loss caused by the tort liability system could be in the range of 28% of the excess transaction costs, or $50 billion per year.

Adding this projected deadweight loss to the conservative measure of tort system inefficiency ($101 billion, a measure that assumes the propriety of noneconomic damages) produces a total inefficiency of $151 billion. Of course, since noneconomic damages are not part of an injured party's compensation (they include pain and suffering and punitive damages) they can also be considered part of the inefficiency. Using a more expansive measure of inefficiency ($158 billion, the measure that assumes that noneconomic damages are inefficient) produces a total inefficiency of $208 billion per year. These figures, of course, include only the tort litigation costs developed from the Tillinghast-Towers Perrin study. When these figures are expanded to include the projected cost of all civil litigation, the absolute inefficiency becomes even greater, resulting in a total inefficiency ranging from $224 billion under the conservative view to $286 billion under the expansive view.

---

18.   *Id.* at 12.

2002 Civil Litigation Inefficiency (Figure 1.4) (All amounts in billions)		
Economic Awards	$76.890	
Noneconomic Awards	$61.512	
Total Economic and Noneconomic Awards	$138.402	
Actual Transaction Costs	$192.225	(See Figure 1.3)
Optimal Transaction Costs[a]	$17.684	
	Direct Inefficiency[d]	Total Inefficiency[e]
Conservative[b]	$174.540	$224.540
Expansive[c]	$236.052	$286.052

Notes

(a) Represents 23% of the economic awards

(b) The conservative inefficiency number assumes that all noneconomic awards are properly granted and are excluded from the measurement of inefficiency.

(c) The expansive number assumes that all noneconomic awards are improperly granted and adds that amount to the measurement of direct inefficiency.

(d) Direct inefficiency is equal to the difference between actual transaction costs and optimal transaction costs.

(e) Total inefficiency, in both the conservative and expensive measures, is the sum of direct inefficiency plus an estimated $50 billion in deadweight loss.

By any measure, the inefficiency in the U.S. litigation system is a substantial sum.

Personalizing the Cost of Litigation

This kind of economic analysis, resulting in an expansive measure of inefficiency of $286 billion per year, is difficult for most of us to comprehend. The number is so large that it is hard to put into perspective. To gain some perspective, the $286 billion Americans spent in 2003 on litigation inefficiency:

• Amounts to approximately $1,014 for every person in the U.S.[19]

• Amounts to nearly 10% of the annual income of an average family.[20]

• Is more than twice the amount spent by Americans on new cars in a year.[21]

• Is more than the entire amount paid in income tax by all of the corporations in the U.S.[22]

• Is more than the entire farm income of the U.S.[23]

Who Pays for the Inefficiency of Litigation?

The costs inherent in litigation must ultimately be borne by one or more of three possible sources: consumers, landowners or the owners of capital.[24] These categories are not mutually exclusive, and some individuals might fall into more than one or even all three categories.

Determining how the cost of litigation is paid is complex because it is not enough to identify who pays the cost legally (i.e., the parties who actually litigate the cases in the system) but who ultimately bears the economic impact of those costs (including both the direct costs and the indirect (or deadweight) costs). Analyzing the distribution of costs is often done in connection with the cost of taxes, since identifying "who pays" is generally a matter of great political interest.

---

19. The most recent estimate of U.S. population (2003) was 290 million. U.S. Census (July 1, 2003) *available at* http://www.census.gov/statab/ranks/rank01.html.
20. Compared to the year 2000 median family income of $41,994. U.S. Census (2000) (providing median income by state) *available at* http://www.census.gov/statab/ranks/rank33.xls.
21. Council of Economic Advisors, Economic Report of the President (Feb. 2004) at 208, *available at* http://www.gpoaccess.gov/usbudget/fy05/pdf/2004_erp.pdf.
22. *Id.* at 389.
23. *Id.* at 396.
24. Council of Economic Advisors, *supra* n12 at 13.

The inquiry can become so complicated, however, that some government agencies avoid the inquiry altogether and others adopt various arbitrary measures. What is important for policy-makers to understand, however, is that in the ultimate sense every American bears the brunt of the litigation "tax".

For example, to the extent that the cost of litigation inefficiency is borne mostly by the producers of goods and services, those costs are added to the prices charged by producers for their products, thereby passing the costs on to consumers. To the extent that the cost of litigation inefficiency reduces the profitability of U.S. firms, that reduction in profits reduces the market value of those firms. For those firms that are publicly traded on the stock market, their stocks trade at a lower value to the extent their profits are reduced by the cost of litigation inefficiency. And, to the extent that Americans own stock in those companies (either directly as stockholders or indirectly through mutual funds or pensions that invest in stocks) that decline in value affects Americans.

Using the lower tort costs of 2001 (and ignoring the effects of contract litigation) the Council of Economic Advisors concluded that the cost of the inefficiency of tort litigation was greater than the year 2000 federal budget for all of the following programs combined: education, training and employment, general science, space and technology, conservation and land management, pollution control and abatement, disaster relief and insurance, community development, federal law enforcement and administration of justice, and unemployment compensation. As that study concluded, "viewed differently, at more than 3 percent of wages per year, the cost of the litigation tax is also far more than enough money to solve Social Security's long-term financing crisis…. [this inefficiency] represents a large drain on the productive resources of the United States."[25]

The Heart of the Problem

So what causes this inefficiency? The answer lies in some of the numbers we've just reviewed. That is, the component parts of the inefficiency consist of:

a.   the costs of claimants, including their attorneys ($66 billion),

b.   the costs of defendants, including their attorneys ($49 billion),

c.   the cost of administration ($76 billion), and

---

25.   *Id.* at 17.

d. perhaps, the costs of noneconomic damage awards ($61 billion). *See* Figure
    1.3.

In other words, litigation as it is conducted in the U.S. today is simply too expensive, both in nominal dollars and in comparison to other methods of conflict resolution.

   This conclusion may not be surprising to many, and yet the solutions that are
often proposed to the litigation crisis often seem to ignore this fundamental
understanding. If litigation is too expensive, policymakers can either adopt rules
to discourage litigation or they can adopt rules that will make litigation cheaper.
And yet, as we'll discuss in the next few chapters, policy-makers have chosen a litigation system that gives economic incentives that induce actors to initiate litigation and maximize the transaction costs of litigation. Doing nothing means
choosing to keep the inefficiency the way it is.

2

How the American Litigation System Works

Considerate men, of every description, ought to prize whatever will tend to beget or fortify that temper in the courts: as no man can be sure that he may not be to-morrow the victim of a spirit of injustice, by which he may be a gainer to-day. And every man must now feel that the inevitable tendency of such a spirit is to sap the foundations of public and private confidence, and to introduce in its stead universal distrust and distress. Federalist No. 78

Before we can examine reforming the U.S. litigation system we need to delve in more detail into its workings. How did we develop a litigation system that generates hundreds of billions of dollars in inefficiency every year? What alternatives exist?

For non-lawyers, this may be an interesting glimpse into a process that is far removed from the glamorous portrayals given in television and movie dramas. For lawyers, however, this may seem like a re-hash of the first year of law school. If you find yourself in that latter category you may want to skip forward to Chapter 3.

The Structure of the Legal System

The American legal system is the product of a number of processes, including the U.S. Constitution, the constitutions of the U.S. states and the so-called "common law". Understanding how the system works requires an understanding of each of these processes.

The "common law" is a term that describes the basic legal concepts at play in most tort and contracts cases.

In medieval England (circa 1200) there were two sources of law: the church and the king. The church's law (or canon law) was based upon the teachings of the medieval Christian church. Offences such as murder, theft, and trespass were handled by canon courts that were typically presided upon by priests acting on the authority of the pope. The king's courts (later called courts of chancery or courts of equity) sought to achieve the "king's justice" and addressed disputes between individuals (or offences against the king) which fell outside the strict rules of the canon courts. Over time, the courts of equity came to represent a procedural attempt to reach rules of fairness in disputes between individuals that were beyond the boundaries of canon law.

After Henry VIII established the Church of England as an institution separate from the Roman Catholic Church (and subject to the English monarch), the English courts fell underneath the rule of the king but, for reasons of tradition, separate courts remained for breaches of the canon law (and these came to be known as "courts of law") and those courts which sought to achieve rules of fairness (which continued to be known as "courts of equity"). Over time, both courts developed rules of law based upon precedent and tradition. Statutes (whether authored by parliament or the king) supplemented the law of precedent from time to time, but the decisional rules created by precedent resolved many issues in both the courts of law and the courts of equity. This body of precedential decision-making became known as the common law.

Early American colonists brought this system of common law to pre-revolutionary America. With the American Revolution and the ratification of the U.S. Constitution in 1789, the court system evolved and incorporated new principles from the Constitution, but the decisional principles of English common law remained. To this day, an education in the common law, including references to pre-revolutionary English common law, is part of the curriculum of most U.S. law schools.

The U.S. Constitution authorized Congress to establish a system of federal courts for the resolution of federal disputes. Article III, Section 1 of the Constitution stipulates merely that "The judicial Power of the United States, shall be vested in one supreme Court, and in such inferior Courts as Congress may from time to time ordain and establish." In practice, the federal court system may have jurisdiction over a case in one of two ways: if the case involves a question of federal law (sometimes called "federal question jurisdiction") and in cases in which the adverse parties are citizens of different states (often called "diversity jurisdiction"). In virtually all other situations—where the legal questions are not based on federal law and where the adverse parties are residents of the same state—jurisdiction is almost always proper in a state court. As a result, roughly 95 percent of all civil cases are filed in state courts and only 5 percent in federal courts.[26]

The federal court system and most state court systems have procedural rules to govern the conduct of civil cases. Civil cases in federal courts are governed by the Federal Rules of Civil Procedure, a statute that was passed through Congress and is occasionally updated.[27]

Each of the U.S. states has a court system that is created by the state's constitution. There are variations in many states, but most have a litigation system that mirrors the federal court system, with trial courts, appellate courts and a supreme court. Likewise, most states have a civil procedural system that is substantively similar to the Federal Rules of Civil Procedure. In many states, in fact, even the section numbers of the states' civil procedural rules are the same as the Federal Rules. In other states, legislatures have used the Federal Rules as a guide but have adopted minor variations.

Many people have a mental concept of courts that is derived in large measure from television and the movies. Popular courtroom dramas often feature conflicts that go from dispute to trial in the space of a single thirty-minute episode. Reality, however, is much slower and involves far less time in the courtroom.

The Civil Litigation Process

Civil litigation takes place in a series of phases, each of which represents an opportunity for the defendant to prevail and avoid liability. At each phase in the litigation process, the court applies a legal standard to determine whether the plaintiff may proceed with its claims or whether those claims should be dismissed. To prevail and obtain an enforceable judgment (or an order for the defendant to pay some amount to the plaintiff) from the court, the plaintiff must prevail in each phase.

The logic behind this process, which is essentially the same on both the state and federal levels, is that as the process moves forward, the plaintiff must satisfy successively higher standards of proof or determination to keep its case viable. Consequently, at the initial stages of litigation a plaintiff need only satisfy the barest legal requirements. At the later stages of the case, the plaintiff must satisfy a higher standard. By requiring successively higher standards of proof, the theory

---

26. Congressional Budget Office, *The Economics of U.S. Tort Liability*, *supra* n4 at viii.
27. The Federal Rules of Civil Procedure (commonly abbreviated as Fed.R.Civ.P.) can be found in Title 28 of the United States Code.

goes, the process weeds out meritless cases in a logical manner. As you will see, however, this logic does not always work efficiently.

Preliminary Motions

A civil case, in most courts, begins with a "complaint".[28] Under the Federal Rules, in the complaint, the plaintiff (the party initiating the lawsuit) must set forth a "short and plain statement of the claim showing that the pleader is entitled to relief."[29] The requirements for a legally adequate complaint are few. The complaint merely needs to allege the minimal requirements to "state a claim".[30] Importantly, the complaint does *not* need to provide *any* evidence that the allegations are true, does *not* need to quantify the plaintiff's damages (or put any dollar value on those damages) and does *not* need to identify any witnesses or otherwise say anything that might bear ultimately on the merits of the case. What then does it mean for a complaint to "state a claim"?

In civil cases, claims represent legally cognizable arguments for relief or, in other words, arguments that are recognized by the law as valid reasons to establish liability against the defendant. Examples of claims include breach of contract, negligence, fraud and other torts that are either established by statute or are part of the common law. "Tort" derives from the Latin word for tortoise, meaning "twisted" and the bulk of the common law in America today consists of the common law of torts.[31] Each cause of action consists of a number of elements. The minimum elements of each cause of action are determined either by statute or by the common law of the applicable court.

---

28. In this book I will be referring to procedural rules used in the federal civil system and in most state courts unless otherwise mentioned. Minor variations may exist in some states, but the general principles described will be consistent in the vast majority of states except in two specific jurisdictions: Louisiana and the District of Columbia. Louisiana is different from the other forty-nine states by virtue of its history as a province of France. (Louisiana was a French possession until 1803 when President Jefferson purchased it in the Louisiana Purchase). The District of Columbia, of course, is not a state but rather a special creature of federal law, governed in significant part by Congress with local control through a mayor and a city council.

29. Fed. R. Civ. P. 8(a).

30. The complaint is not limited to the elements of a claim under existing law but may also allege the elements of a claim that represents a "good faith argument for the…establishment of new law." *See* Fed. R. Civ. P. 11. The importance of this distinction will become clear later.

For example, in a case in which the plaintiff alleges that the defendant is liable for the tort of negligence, the plaintiff must allege that: (a) the defendant owed the plaintiff a duty of care, (b) the defendant failed to fulfill (or "breached") that duty of care, (c) the defendant's breach of care was the cause of the plaintiff's damages and (d) the plaintiff in fact suffered damages.

Each element of the claim can be subjected to scrutiny and measured against the prior decisions of the court in a preliminary motion by the defendant. Importantly, however, a defendant's preliminary motion can only challenge the elements of the claims pled by the plaintiff and not the ultimate truth or falsity of the claims. While skillful defense counsel can sometimes succeed at dismissing all or a portion of a case through preliminary motions, the standard applied by the trial court at the preliminary motion stage is very precise and tends to favor the plaintiff. The trial court is required to determine whether all of the plaintiff's allegations are sufficient, standing alone, to add up to a legally cognizable claim. The trial court (with only a few exceptions) cannot consider any evidence the defendant might want to present but is strictly limited to the allegations of the plaintiff.

Let's examine these concepts in a basic example. Imagine that you are driving down the road and come to a stop sign. You stop properly but the driver behind you fails to stop and hits the back end of your car, denting your bumper. (You later get a quote from an auto repair shop to repair the dent for $200). Would you be able to sue the other driver for negligence? Looking at the four elements of negligence, probably so. The driver owed you a duty of care (the duty to obey the rules of the road and not to hit other drivers); the driver breached that duty by failing to stop and by hitting your car; it was the driver's failure to stop that caused the dent to your car and the dent itself is an injury to you; it will cost you $200 to repair it. Under these facts, if you sued the other driver, the other driver probably would not have much chance of dismissing your claims at the preliminary motion stage of the case.

Let's change the facts a little. Assume that everything transpired exactly as before, except that the collision between the cars resulted in no dent at all. You suffer no physical or other injuries and there is no damage to your car. If you sued

---

31. In theory, a tort is a wrongful action that any reasonable person should recognize as wrong without the benefit of legal training. Torts consist of virtually all causes of action in private litigation other than breach of contract, certain specialized claims and claims that are authorized by statute. Another tool of memorization helpful to law students is the saying that tort can be defined in three words: "actionable civil wrong."

the other driver anyway (perhaps just because you were angry or because you hoped a jury trial would teach the other driver a lesson) the other driver might succeed in dismissing your case on a preliminary motion. In this example, your case is missing one of the four elements of a proper negligence claim. Even if you proved everything that you claim to be true (the driver owed a duty, the driver breached the duty and the driver hit your car) you still cannot claim to have suffered any damages. As a result, if you sued the other driver the court should grant the other driver's preliminary motion to dismiss. The law simply doesn't give you a right to sue because you're angry or want to teach someone "a lesson". The case should be dismissed because one of the claim's essential elements—that the plaintiff suffered damages in fact—is missing.

The limitations on preliminary motions are important from a defendant's point of view. At this stage, the defendant has been served with a complaint and almost certainly has hired a lawyer. Most defense lawyers work by the hour, so the defendant is incurring substantial costs. A preliminary motion to dismiss a complaint for failing to state a claim will generally require at least several dozen hours of legal work (learning the background of the case, reviewing any available documents or evidence, researching the law and preparing a memorandum of legal research in support of the motion to dismiss). Consequently, an extremely lucky defendant who is able to dispose of a complaint in a very simple case with a preliminary motion to dismiss might only have to pay for 50 to 100 billable hours. Depending on the lawyer's hourly rate, the work could amount to $10-40,000.

In this preliminary stage of civil litigation, after the plaintiff files its complaint, the defendant must either file a preliminary motion (challenging whether the complaint has stated a claim on which relief can be granted) or file an answer. Timing may vary slightly, but most courts allow a defendant only thirty days in which either to file a preliminary motion or an answer. If the defendant files a preliminary motion, the plaintiff will have an opportunity to file written arguments in opposition to the motion and the defendant may thereafter have the chance to submit a written rebuttal. At this point, after the motion, opposition and any supplementary arguments are before the court, the case may be in procedural limbo. Few courts have any procedural rules to compel judges to keep any particular pace and it is not uncommon for judges to allow fully-briefed motions to remain pending for months before taking action.

In acting on a preliminary motion, the judge may invite the parties to a hearing before the court or the court may simply act upon the parties' papers. Again, at this preliminary stage, a hearing before the court will only involve the arguments of the parties' lawyers. The court is not concerned with the truth or falsity of the plaintiff's claims but only with the legal sufficiency of the plaintiff's complaint and whether, if all of the allegations were true and taken in the light most favorable to the plaintiff, it would be possible for the plaintiff to win.

This fact highlights one of the procedural problems with the American litigation system. A plaintiff who is able to file a legally sufficient complaint can compel any defendant, large or small, rich or poor, to incur the expense of hiring an attorney and bearing all of the other costs and inconveniences of participating in litigation without any need to prove the truth of the plaintiff's claims. Even worse, an unscrupulous plaintiff (or even one who is willing to shade or bend the truth in his claims) can use the power of the legal system to force costs upon an unwilling defendant.

And again, from another point of view, because the litigation process does not impose any requirement of reasonability upon a plaintiff or force a plaintiff to take into account whether the totality of the litigation process will be worth the costs it will impose on both parties, an unwise plaintiff may commence litigation (even where his own interests will be harmed in the long run) and compel the defendant to bear nearly all the cost. Many defense lawyers have had to sit through conferences with their defendant clients who have exclaimed, "But how can he [the plaintiff] do this? I did nothing wrong and I can prove it" only to have to tell their clients:

> "You may be right and you may ultimately prevail, but the process does not allow us to 'fast forward' to the end game. You will be forced to bear the cost and burden of litigation until you have an opportunity—at the trial—to present the evidence that will relieve you from liability. And, if you win, although you'll owe the plaintiff nothing, you will have no ability to recover from anyone what you have spent in attorneys' fees and costs."

If the defendant does not elect to file a preliminary motion to dismiss (or if the court denies the defendant's preliminary motion) the defendant must file an answer. In most courts, the defendant's answer is a dull affair and contains even less real information about the case than the plaintiff's complaint. The defendant's answer must, paragraph by paragraph, either admit or deny the allegations in the complaint (or, if the defendant lacks the information to either admit or deny, to say so). Importantly, though, while the defendant's answer will either admit or deny key facts, it need not (and usually cannot) "prove" anything. Evidence is not involved. All that matters in an answer is the admission or denial of allegations.

For example, if the first paragraph of the plaintiff's complaint states, "Defendant Acme Corporation is a Delaware corporation with a place of business at 101 Main Street, Akron, Ohio", the defendant will address each factual allegation in this paragraph. If, for example, the complaint got the mailing address correct but incorrectly identified Acme's state of incorporation, paragraph one of the answer might state, "Defendant admits that it has a place of business at 101 Main Street, Akron Ohio but denies all of the remaining allegations in Paragraph 1 of Plaintiff's complaint." Some civil complaints can be as short as twenty or thirty paragraphs. Others may run for hundreds of paragraphs. Consequently, it is not uncommon for an answer to run over many pages, carefully repeating and admitting the truthful allegations and denying or taking no position on the remaining allegations.

The mind-numbing repetition of factual claims in the defendant's answer often appears pointless to non-lawyers (and there are good arguments that the process could be streamlined) but it does tend to reduce the number of facts in contention by forcing the defendant carefully either to admit or deny particular facts.

Discovery

Discovery is the process by which litigants use the compulsory power of the court to compel each other—and unrelated third parties—to disclose documents and information to each other. In most courts, discovery can begin once the defendant is served with the complaint (i.e., even before the defendant files a preliminary motion or an answer). Through the discovery process, each party to the case is able to collect information that may lead to the development of evidence in the case.

Discovery can take many forms. Parties to a case may compel each other to submit to a deposition, produce documents, permit their offices or assets to be examined or inspected, answer written questions, admit in writing facts that are undisputed and identify those documents or witnesses that they believe support their positions.

In a deposition the parties meet informally, usually in a lawyer's offices, in the presence of a licensed court reporter (or stenographer). No judge or jury is present, but the person whose deposition is being taken, is sworn (or put under oath) by the court reporter and is questioned by the attorneys for the parties. In litigation between individuals, each individual can be required to submit to a deposition. In cases involving a corporation, the corporation's directors, employees and other representatives can be required to submit to a deposition.

Parties to a case can also compel unrelated third parties to submit to a deposition by using the court's power to issue a subpoena. While the subpoena, in theory, issues from the court (and violating the terms of the subpoena can subject the violator to criminal sanctions through the court's contempt power) the subpoena is actually prepared by the attorney for one of the parties and simply filed with the court for its records.

A deposition can, by itself, be an uncomfortable affair. Depending on the issues in the case, the questions can be fairly personal and precise, asking the witness about specific claims and particular documents or pieces of evidence.

In addition to depositions, the parties to litigation may also require each other to answer written questions (called interrogatories) and provide relevant documents (in response to a request for the production of documents). In a deposition of a non-party witness, the witness may also be required by the subpoena to provide documents or information related to the case.

In cases involving businesses the process of producing documents for discovery can be especially arduous since the attorneys have both an ethical and a legal obligation to ensure that they have produced *all* of the documents that are relevant to the opposing party's request. In a claim involving a manufacturer's liability for a product it produced, a request for documents might ask for "all documents pertaining to the defendant's design and engineering of the product". A request like this might appear simple, but could effectively require the defendant's attorneys to interview hundreds of company employees (who might be spread out across the country) to ensure that the attorneys identified all of the responsive documents. Identifying the documents could take months and generate massive attorneys' fees.

Importantly, the discovery process is intended to be informal. The Federal Rules of Civil Procedure allow parties to obtain any information, documents or testimony that is "reasonably calculated to lead to the discovery of admissible evidence." Experienced attorneys know that judges hate to preside over disputes involving discovery and usually go to great lengths to resolve their disputes without involving the judge. And yet, this very liberal concept of discovery increases the cost and burden of litigation on the parties (not to mention non-parties) at a preliminary stage of the litigation and often before the court has had any chance to consider the merits of the complaint.

The length and cost of discovery in a civil case can vary greatly. In small civil cases, the parties may take few, if any, depositions. In larger or more complicated disputes, especially in those involving a corporate defendant with a number of employees who may know something about the dispute, discovery can last for months or even years. A defendant in such a small civil case might make it through the discovery stage with legal fees of $15-30,000. In a larger case, legal fees and expenses can amount to $1 million or more.

An alert reader might begin to see how the liberal American litigation system has an institutional bias towards plaintiffs. A plaintiff can file a complaint and force a defendant to participate in litigation—including discovery that can last for many months—incurring legal fees in the tens or hundreds of thousands of dollars all before any court considers the fundamental merits of the plaintiff's case (or even whether the subject of the complaint merits the expense that is being forced upon the defendant).

As with the filing of the complaint itself, there is nothing a defendant can do to avoid incurring substantial expense if a plaintiff is determined to exercise all of its discovery rights. Although the Federal Rules do purport to discourage unnecessary discovery and require the parties to avoid discovery that is merely duplicative or is more expensive or burdensome than some alternative means, the fundamental rule of discovery makes it very difficult to cut short the process. The fundamental rule that a party is entitled to discover any documents or testimony "reasonably calculated to lead to the discovery of admissible evidence" allows a plaintiff who can construct any reasonable theory to overcome a defendant's motion to cut short or limit discovery.

Summary Judgment

Eventually the discovery process will come to a close. In some courts local rules limit discovery to a certain period of time. (Six months is fairly standard). In other courts the parties may be required to report to the judge on their progress periodically and the judge may impose a schedule on the parties. Nevertheless, in most jurisdictions, the period of time from filing of the complaint to the close of discovery usually runs for about one year. It is not uncommon, however, for this period to last for several years.

The close of discovery allows the defendant another opportunity to dismiss the plaintiff's complaint and avoid liability. Through a summary judgment motion, the plaintiff may ask the court to dismiss the plaintiff's claims, looking at the totality of the evidence that has been gleaned through the discovery process. Even at this point, however, the standard a defendant must overcome to gain a dismissal is very high. Under Federal Rule 56, the court may dismiss a party's claim only if there is *no* "genuine issue of material fact" *and* all of the admissible evidence, taken in the light most favorable to the party making the claim, would be insufficient to allow a reasonable jury to find in favor of that party. Although defendants often try to use motions for summary judgment to dismiss the claims of plaintiffs, in a case where a defendant has counterclaims pending against a plaintiff, the plaintiff may also use summary judgment to try to dismiss the counterclaim. The rule for dismissal at summary judgment is the same, regardless of whether it is the plaintiff or the defendant who is making the motion.

Although this standard sounds similar to the standard involved at the preliminary motion stage, it is different in that the judge on a motion for summary judgment is allowed (actually, required) to look at the evidence. What is similar, however, is the bias given in favor of the party who is opposing summary judgment. (Although the party opposing summary judgment is often the plaintiff, the Federal Rules actually speak of the "movant" and the "non-movant" because the plaintiff can move for summary judgment against the defendant's counterclaims in the same way that the defendant might move against the plaintiff's primary claims). If there is *any* theory of the case that is possible under the available evidence in which a reasonable jury *could* find in the non-movant's favor, the judge is required by the rules to *deny* the motion.

Technically, a defendant need not wait to the close of discovery to file a summary judgment motion. Because the rules require the court to deny summary judgment if there is any theory of the case in which the non-movant could win, however, the non-movant will generally respond by claiming that it will produce evidence during discovery that will be sufficient. Judges are often inclined to deny summary judgment when a plaintiff can plausibly claim that it will be able to come up with enough evidence to keep its claim viable. Even if that evidence is not yet apparent, the plaintiff can claim that there is a "genuine issue of material fact" concerning that evidence and such assertions are sometimes enough to keep the case alive, at least for awhile. The consequence, however, is that a party who is pursuing a fatally weak claim can keep that claim alive long enough to drag its opponent through a long and costly discovery process.

Preparing a summary judgment motion is a difficult task for the defense lawyer. In a complex civil case in which there have been a dozen or more depositions and hundreds, or even thousands, of pages of documentary evidence, the defendant's lawyer must cull through these thousands of pages to find the *best evidence favoring* the plaintiff. Then, in its written arguments for summary judgment, the defense lawyer must show have even the plaintiff's best evidence cannot be enough for a reasonable jury to reach a plaintiff's verdict. In doing this, the defendant is not able to argue questions of credibility. If the plaintiff's best evidence of the defendant's wrongdoing is the deposition testimony of a biased or unreliable witness, that evidence will usually be enough to deny the defendant's motion. To prevail, the defendant needs to pull off the difficult trick of showing how there is no logical combination of available evidence that is sufficient to allow a reasonable jury to reach a plaintiff's verdict.

It is at the summary judgment stage that most high-value civil litigation is won or lost. The upshot of losing a motion for summary judgment is that the plaintiff gets to present his case to a jury. The trial process, as explained below, is both risky and expensive. Many corporate defendants will perceive risk and expense to trying the merits of a case and will be pressured to settle with the plaintiff if they cannot dispose of a case at summary judgment.

And yet, it takes so little for a plaintiff to survive a summary judgment motion. The plaintiff doesn't need to have a good case, or even a case that is worth litigating. Rather, the plaintiff merely needs to cobble together a complaint with the minimum requirements to survive a preliminary motion and collect enough evidence so that there is at least one theory of the case by which a reasonable jury can reach a plaintiff's verdict.

Trial

Many studies and works on the American litigation system have focused on the role of jury trials. The jury trial system in the U.S. is somewhat unusual. The constitutions of many states guarantee plaintiffs a trial before a jury in a civil case. Most other common law jurisdictions outside the U.S., however, conduct civil trials in front of a judge alone who acts both as the arbiter of legal questions as well as factual questions. Because of this oddity in American law, and some of the errors and horror stories civil juries have created, advocates of reform have focused a lot of attention on the role of juries.

By the time a civil case reaches trial, it has been pending for many months and perhaps years. In the smallest and simplest civil cases, a defendant may have expended only tens of thousands in attorneys' fees. In larger civil cases, a defendant may have expended hundreds of thousands or even millions of dollars.

Most courts have procedural requirements that force the parties to organize their cases in advance through a pre-trial order. In the pre-trial process the parties may submit outlines of their principle arguments and summarize the expected testimony of their witnesses for the judge. The judge may then schedule the trial for a number of days based upon the parties' outlines and requests for time. Pre-trial procedures can vary significantly between courts, however, and some courts have minimalist requirements that allow trials to go on with little limitation and with the maximum potential for surprise.

And this brings us to the role of juries. In federal courts and most state courts civil cases are tried before a jury. The jury may consist of as many as twelve or as few as six persons. In some cases, the parties will agree to try the case before the judge in what is called a "bench trial". In either situation, whether the case is tried before a jury or the judge, the judge or jury acts as the "factfinder" with the primary role of determining questions of fact and questions of witness credibility. While the judge in a jury case will defer to the jury's opinion on what happened in the case (i.e., what facts are established based upon the testimony of the various witnesses) the judge will always retain responsibility for determining the law (i.e., whether a particular set of facts leads to a finding of liability in favor of one party or another). While the distinction between questions of fact and questions of law is a difficult one and generally takes several weeks out of your first year in law school, it is not terribly important for the issues in this book.

What is important, however, is the understanding that questions of law are the only questions that a court will resolve in the stages of the proceedings that lead up to trial. Virtually all factual questions remain unresolved until trial. If a defendant is sued in a civil case the only way for the defendant to have the case dismissed before trial is through a dispositive motion that depends upon a purely legal issue. To prevail on a purely legal issue, a party must be able to convince the court that even if all of the facts are as the other party claims, the law would still require that the other party lose. If the defendant believes it is not liable for any other reason there is no way to short circuit the system prior to trial. There is no way to expedite the process to bring the case to trial any sooner than the process would otherwise require.

To take an example, let's imagine that someone (we'll call him Mr. Evil) sues you for stealing his car. Well, actually, your car. Let's assume that Mr. Evil files a suit saying that the car that is sitting in your garage (the keys for which are in your pocket and the title for which is in your name in your desk drawer) is actually his. Let's assume that Mr. Evil is willing to lie in the complaint. (Mr. Evil would have to be lying; I just described your car). Your defense is that Mr. Evil is lying. You can prove that he is lying because the title is in your name. You can produce three dozen witnesses who saw you purchase and pay for the car. You can produce all of the paperwork from the dealer where you bought the car. You will *not* be able to dismiss this case in a preliminary motion. You *might* be able to dismiss the case in a summary judgment motion (different courts have different standards on the level of proof required at summary judgment). If you didn't win dismissal at summary judgment, you would need to go through the entire litigation process all the way to trial before you could prove that Mr. Evil was lying. That process could easily take months and perhaps even longer than a year.

At the trial of this hypothetical car theft case, as the plaintiff, Mr. Evil would probably be able to insist upon a trial by jury. You would produce all of the evidence described above to show that you were the real owner of the car. Mr. Evil would do his best to cast doubt on your truthfulness. If Mr. Evil was able to persuade the jury that you (and not he) were lying—for example, if the jury was persuaded by Mr. Evil's slick presentation or if you looked nervous and untrustworthy to the eyes of the jury—Mr. Evil might actually succeed in suing you for stealing your own car.

Although they will never admit it publicly, most attorneys have a relatively low opinion of juries. Even plaintiffs' attorneys (who generally champion the rights of plaintiffs to have jury trials) favor juries not because they believe them to be terribly wise or capable to discerning truth from falsehood. On the contrary, very often plaintiffs' attorneys wager that they will be able to inflame the jury into a desire to punish the defendant either through an appeal to the jury's sympathy (for the injured plaintiff) or its antipathy (aimed at the defendant's wrongdoing). For most plaintiffs' attorneys, the litigation process before trial is an undesirable but unavoidable hurdle to overcome before "spinning the prize wheel" in seeking a jury verdict at trial.

As anyone who has been through the jury duty process knows, must jurors are unhappy to be involved in the legal system. Most jury pools are selected from voter registration rolls, so most jurors are employed and tend to have all of the time-constraints of responsible adults. A prospective juror receives a jury summons in the mail (usually written in a confusing style that requires several readings before its purpose becomes clear). On the appointed day (after clearing his or her calendar, taking care of any personal appointments and scheduling the time off from employment) the juror must make his or her way to the courthouse (often for the first time) and sign in with the court. Many courts give jurors a hand-out or brochure that describes the jury system and reminds jurors of their patriotic duty to serve on the jury and some subject jurors to an introductory film or video that has all the appeal of a high school civics lesson.

By the time the juror arrives to a particular courtroom to be considered for the jury on a particular case, the juror is unhappy and wishing with all his might that he will be rejected so that he can go home and resume his life.

At the commencement of the trial, the judge will guide the attorneys through the "voir dire" process in which the attorneys will question prospective jurors in an attempt to weed out any jurors who have any demonstrable bias to one of the parties or who the attorney otherwise believes may be inclined against his client. Depending on the local rules of the court, prospective jurors with some demonstrable bias (a juror who is related to a party, employed by a party or who otherwise expresses some kind of bias) will often be excused "for cause". Attorneys can dismiss other prospective jurors peremptorily (by peremptory challenge) if they fit a profile that the attorney thinks may be inclined against his party.

Volumes have been written on the art or science of picking jurors. Wealthy litigants may even employ jury consultants (often sociologists or psychologists with specialized training in psychological profiling) to assist the attorneys in stacking the deck with favorable jurors. It is not clear what impact such extraordinary measures may have, but it is telling that they exist at all. After all, if the civil trial process is supposed to be a fair opportunity for the parties to present their versions of the facts, why should the psychological profiles of the jurors matter? Attempting to influence the process by excluding certain types of jurors who fit a profile would seem to undermine the concept of fairness that ought to motivate a jury trial system. Admitting that the system is capable of being influenced suggests that it is not fair at all but is rather an elaborate (and expensive) game that can be won through a slick manipulation of a juror's biases and predispositions.

In the hypothetical case where Mr. Evil sued you (wrongly, of course) for stealing your own car, how comfortable would you be in trusting your fate to a jury of strangers? Is there anything about you that you think might bias the jury against you? Is Mr. Evil well known in the community where this jury lives? Are you? Is Mr. Evil good-looking or likely to be appealing to the jury? Are you? As you can see, taking your case to trial can be a matter of significant risk even when you are entirely in the right.

Juries have figured prominently in film and television portrayals of civil trials and for that reason tend to animate the minds of many Americans when they think of the trial system. In *Runaway Jury*, for example, a movie based on a novel by the lawyer-turned-author John Grisham, two survivors of a small town shooting spree, through an elaborate ruse, conspire to put one of them on the jury in a trial concerning the liability of a gun manufacturer in a similar shooting. Although the conspirators' motives don't become clear to the audience until the final frames, the movie casts them as the heroes as they try to manipulate the jury to favor the plaintiff against the evil forces of the gun manufacturing industry. While the conspirators break numerous laws in their attempt to affect the outcome of the case, the movie paints them as heroes. And yet, as the trailer for the movie proclaims, "trials are too important to be decided by juries."

The jury's role in a civil case is to determine only questions of fact. The judge's role is to determine all questions of law. In the pre-trial motions in the litigation leading up to trial, the parties had the opportunity to narrow the legal issues involved. In the preliminary motion stage, the defendant had the opportunity to ask the court to dismiss claims that were insufficient—as a matter of law—to amount to a valid claim. If the court did its job, there should be no legally invalid claims left by the time the case goes to trial. Likewise, at the summary judgment stage, the defendant had the chance to ask the court to dismiss any claims for which there was not enough evidence for a reasonable fact-finder to find for the plaintiff. Again, if the court did its job, there should be no claims of this variety remaining. All that should remain, in theory, are those legally valid claims for which there is sufficient evidence for a reasonable fact-finder to find in favor of the plaintiff.

Throughout this discussion, I've written that "if the court does its job" and "in theory" certain claims should be dismissed. All human creations, including courts, are fallible and courts sometimes don't do their jobs well and processes don't operate in reality as they should in theory. This introduces a level of uncertainty to the process and to the decision-making of both the plaintiff and the defendant. A judge who is uncertain, or who fears the political implications of dismissing a case, may simply let a case that ought to be dismissed "go to the jury".

But, in theory, the jury should hear the evidence provided by the parties and make key determinations of fact. The trial will usually begin with some preliminary statements by the judge. The judge will tell the jury to set aside any personal biases they may have and to listen carefully to the witnesses. The judge will describe the trial process for the jury and will let the jury know that their job will be to determine the key facts.

Most civil jury trials last a few days. Rare cases may last a single day or may stretch on for many days or weeks. At the conclusion of the trial, after the attorneys have made their closing statements, the judge will charge the jury. As part of the judge's charge, the judge will tell the jury what facts they need to find in their deliberations. In some states, the charge may include a written form for the jurors to complete that tracks the allegations in the case on an issue-by-issue basis. In other states the charge may ask only for the jury's ultimate determination of liability.

During the pre-trial hearing (or at another hearing out of the presence of the jury) the opposing attorneys and the judge will have resolved the factual questions to be determined by the jury. In general, the factual issues will trace the legal requirements of the causes of action the plaintiff is pursuing. For example, in a case in which the plaintiff claims the defendant is liable for breach of contract, the key factual questions may be something like:

a.   Were the defendant (Mr. Jones) and the plaintiff (Mr. Smith) parties to a contract?

b.   If so, did that contract consist of (1) the written document entitled, "Sale Agreement" dated January 15, 1999 or (2) the oral agreement between the parties that Mr. Smith described in his testimony?

c.   If there was a contract between the parties, did that contract obligate Mr. Smith to deliver the goods to Mr. Jones before April 1, 1999?

d.   If there was a contract between the parties, did Mr. Smith in fact fail to deliver the goods to Mr. Jones before April 1, 1999?

e.   If there was a contract between the parties, and you have answered questions (c) and (d) in the affirmative, did Mr. Smith suffer any damages as a consequence of Mr. Jones's failure to deliver the goods before April 1, 1999?

f.   If the answer to question (e) was in the affirmative, what was the dollar value of the damages suffered by Mr. Smith?

As you can see, this jury charge outlines the factual requirements of a claim of breach of contract by identifying if there was a contract, and, if so, what were the terms of the contract, were those terms breached and, if so, what damages resulted. In a simplified example like this, the jury charge gives the jury an outline for their deliberations and forces the jury to consider only the evidence that the court determines is relevant to the matter.

After being charged, the jury retires to deliberate. Juries can deliberate for minutes or for days. Barring the rare situation where the jury cannot reach a verdict[32], after some deliberations the jury returns with a verdict that is then read by the court.

Judgment and Post-Trial Motions

After reading the jury's verdict, the lawyers and the judge are left behind to obtain a final judgment and deal with any post-trial motions. Remember that it is the province of the judge to determine the law and the jury to determine the facts. If the judge believes that the jury reached conclusions that it could not reasonably have reached based upon the evidence brought out at trial, the judge may set aside the jury's verdict and enter judgment in favor of the defendant. In essence, a post-trial order to set aside the jury's verdict is the same as an order granting a motion for summary judgment.[33] In such an order, the judge is ruling that, based upon the facts in evidence, taken in the light most favorable to the plaintiff, there is no way that a reasonable jury could have found in the plaintiff's favor.

Appeal

After the court enters a final judgment, the losing party may appeal. The appellate process differs between state and federal courts but, in general, the losing party has two basic approaches. A party who lost at trial (who is called the "appellant" in the appeals process) must either argue that: (a) there was not enough evidence for the judge or the jury to find in favor of the plaintiff or (b) the judge made errors of law that caused the outcome to be flawed.

---

32. In most states a verdict in a civil case merely needs to be by majority vote. As a result, it is extremely rare for a civil jury to be deadlocked as sometimes happens in criminal trials.

33. In older cases, this kind of post-trial court order is sometimes called a "directed verdict" or described by the Latin phrase, judgment "*non obstantio verdicto*" (judgment notwithstanding the verdict). In 1991, the Federal Rules of Civil Procedure were amended to eliminate these old-fashioned terms, replacing them with the phrase "judgment as a matter of law". *See* Fed. R. Civ. P. 50. In any event, the legal standard for what was formerly a directed verdict is today the same for a judgment as a matter of law, whether the court's order is issued at the pre-trial summary judgment phase (and handled under Rule 56) or as a post-trial judgment as a matter of law (under Rule 50).

When an appellant appeals over issues of fact, the appellant is essentially asking the appellate court to substitute itself for the trial judge in making the fact-intensive determination involved in the summary judgment and post-trial judgment motions. In these kinds of appeals, the standard of review is very high. Appellate courts will usually overturn a trial court's rulings on fact issues only where the appellate court believes the trial court was clearly in error.

On issues of law, however, appellate courts consider the case "de novo".[34] If the appellant can convince the appellate court that the trial court incorrectly ruled on a legal matter—and that the incorrect legal ruling altered the outcome of the case—the appellate court will reverse the ruling and send or ("remand") the case back to the trial court.

Let's return, for example, to the case where Mr. Evil sued you for stealing your own car. Of course, Mr. Evil was lying. The car is yours and you can prove it with documentary evidence (your certificate of title and other paperwork that proves your ownership) and with testimonial evidence (the testimony of your several dozen friends who have seen you treat the car as your own for a long time). If you had sought to have the case dismissed through a preliminary motion (where the only issue is whether the plaintiff has alleged all of the legally-necessary elements of his claim) and if the trial court had granted your motion, dismissing Mr. Evil's case, Mr. Evil could appeal. Even though, as a matter of fact you are in the right, Mr. Evil's claim (though false) is not legally insufficient and the trial court should *not* have granted your preliminary motion. If Mr. Evil appealed, the appellate court *should reverse* the trial court's ruling and order the trial court to let the case go forward. Even though the trial court's action in dismissing the case might have been the "right thing to do" it would have been the wrong decision as a legal matter because the court should not consider questions of credibility (i.e., which party is lying and which is telling the truth) at the preliminary motion stage.

If the losing party prevails on appeal, the appellate court will issue its ruling along with an order that tells the trial court how to proceed. In cases where the appellate court is correcting an error of law, the appellate court may direct the trial court to hold the trial over again, with a new jury, applying the new legal standard set forth by the appellate court. If the appellate court is reversing the

---

34. Latin, "as if new". On issues reviewed *de novo*, the appellate court will overturn the lower court's ruling if it is incorrect, without giving any deference to the legal opinion of the lower court.

trial court's ruling on a factual issue, it may simply direct the trial court to enter judgment accordingly.

Conflicts in the Civil Litigation Process

Each stage in the civil litigation process puts parties in conflict with one another against the backdrop of several premises. The parties (the plaintiff and defendant), of course, are in conflict with one another. After all, it was some kind of conflict that prompted the plaintiff to file a complaint to begin the lawsuit.

The parties are in conflict with the court. In the federal system, judges are appointed by the President and serve for life. In the state systems, judges may be either elected or appointed by the state governors. Whether they plan to run for re-election or have lifetime tenure, however, most judges are motivated by a desire to be right and to avoid being overturned on appeal. Legal newspapers and public interest groups keep statistics on the reversal rates of trial judges. In some jurisdictions, judges can be evaluated both on their reversal rates and on the speed with which they move cases through their courts.

Judges also tend to be motivated by a sense of history and personal prestige. Because they deal with legal precedents on a daily basis, judges are keenly aware of how their decisions can have impacts that last far into history. Many judges sought a place on the bench because they had a personal bent towards "making law" and often see themselves as taking part in a process they believe is important. As a consequence, judges often place a great emphasis on the value of the process in which they are engaged. At times, that procedural value may even surpass the personal or pecuniary concerns that drove the litigants to court in the first place.

The litigation system also reveals conflict between the judicial branch of government generally and its executive and legislative branches. The legislative branch, generally speaking, makes laws with the intention of codifying public policy. For example, if the legislature wants to eliminate or penalize a kind of behavior, the legislature can pass a law imposing tort liability on parties that engage in that kind of behavior and cause damage to others. All of those laws, however, must ultimately be interpreted by courts and enforced by private litigants in actual cases. This can create a tension between the public policy goals that the legislature intended to pursue in a particular statute and the actual outcomes that result from the enforcement of that statute.

The litigation process, however, is intended to take two or more parties with an actual dispute and to force those parties to narrow the scope of their dispute. The narrowing process begins with the preliminary motions, which discard claims that are legally invalid, and continues into the pre-trial motions, which discard claims that lack sufficient evidence to sustain them through trial.

While this process of narrowing issues is logical it does have its drawbacks. In particular, in the situation of factually frivolous claims (like Mr. Evil's car theft case, for example) unless the defendant can find a way to dispose of the case through a purely legal issue, the defendant is stuck with having to go through the entire litigation process all the way to trial. In a legally frivolous case (where the plaintiff purports to rely on a theory of liability that does not exist in the law) the defendant's ability to obtain a dismissal will depend on the judge's personal sense of justice and whether the judge wants to experiment with the plaintiff's novel theory. The litigation process is both time-consuming and expensive. It involves not only giving testimony and producing documents relevant to the claims at hand but also gives the parties a wide-ranging ability to investigate each other's affairs. That investigation can include questioning family, friends, neighbors and co-workers and requiring the parties to produce documents that can be confidential, sensitive and embarrassing. A defendant who is the victim of a frivolous claim has no choice but to spend substantial sums on legal fees in defending itself.

In addition to the imposition of time and expense, becoming a party to litigation can have other substantial impacts. A corporate defendant can see a huge drop in the value of its stock—sometimes even dwarfing its potential liability in the suit—simply from the public relations impact of being sued. An individual who is sued may find herself unable to get financing (like a home mortgage loan) and may be unable to get insurance because underwriters may perceive the litigation as a risk. All of these impositions—time, money, loss of equity, loss of credit, loss of insurance—are costs borne solely by the defendant without hope of reimbursement. Defendants bear these burdens because, so far at least, Congress and the legislatures have chosen that it should be this way. That is, our elected legislators have chosen that it is more important for plaintiffs to have a "right" to explore their claims and grievances through a long and costly court process than for defendants to be free from having these costs imposed upon them. Whether you find this choice reassuring or not depends in large part on whether you anticipate that you might one day be a plaintiff or a defendant.

The system shifts nearly all of the costs, in time, money and inconvenience, onto defendants. Plaintiffs have the power—given them by the laws made by our legislatures—to determine when and how they will use the power of the government to force a defendant into litigation. Plaintiffs have the power to impose costs on defendants, without any responsibility for the propriety of those costs and without any responsibility to determine whether the costs are "worth it". That choice is out of balance.

As you'll see, this very fact—the cost and burden of the litigation process and the inevitability of those costs and burdens once the process starts—drives a great deal of the decision-making made by both sides in litigation. Understanding how parties make decisions and the incentives that drive litigation will make clear why the U.S. litigation system is out of balance and how that imbalance creates more than $286 billion of inefficiency every year.

3

Modeling Incentives to Litigate

Every expansion of private lawyers' power to claim to represent the interests of large groups of clients—through class actions, aggregative methods, and fictions of government representation—was sold as a way to "let the people in"...The much more unambiguous function of class-action suits was to further empower lawyers themselves, who could now demand a great deal more money...secure in the knowledge that their supposed constituents would not be in a position to fire them. Walter Olson, THE RULE OF LAWYERS (2004).

I went to law school at the George Washington University in Washington, D.C. At the time, Jack Friedenthal was the dean and he used to greet incoming students with a speech at the beginning of first year orientation. In his introduction, he described how the common law worked from a series of precedents and how, over time, subsequent judicial decisions shaped the boundaries of the law. He said that these precedents were like stars in the nighttime sky. Each one was a bright point of light with a distinct existence and boundary. In between two or more stars, however, there was darkness. The closer you came to a star, the brighter and clearer it became. His analogy, he explained, described the value of precedents as they related to resolving disputes. In a dispute that was described perfectly by a prior precedent, there was complete clarity: the parties would know how a court would resolve their dispute and there would be no need to litigate. In a dispute that was nowhere near any prior precedent, there was no bright line to determine the outcome. In such a dispute, where it was difficult or impossible to predict the litigated outcome, the parties would be tempted to litigate because either party could imagine an outcome in which it was victorious.

This analogy, I think, describes the fundamental importance of the role of uncertainty in any attempt to analyze the litigation system. The greater the uncertainty of outcome the more likely litigation will ensue.

41

The Economics of Disputes

When I refer to a model in this book, I am referring to an abstract method for assessing the decision-making rationales of parties to a dispute. The model, however, is nothing more than abstract. It will suggest that a party will act on the basis of certain variables. Some might be tempted to describe those variables with the precision of mathematics, but I wouldn't go so far. Doing so suggests a level of precision that is deceptive. Human decision making is never precise and the model I propose should work in most cases, but may not work in all cases, given the infinite number of variables that might work on a particular decision maker in a particular case. Although I think my assumptions about what variables are relevant are reasonable, some may disagree. If my assumptions about what variables to include in the model are not accurate, the model will yield inaccurate results.

In addition, litigation decisions are often made by organizations that are represented in the litigation. Organizations can make decisions in a variety of different ways and different organizations may have different processes or traditions for making decisions. Publicly traded corporate defendants often make decisions with a view toward their quarterly earnings reports. If the quarter is going well, a corporate defendant may have additional cash with which to settle a case without affecting its published earnings. Individual parties to litigation can be affected by their individual budget needs. Plaintiffs' attorneys are often affected by their need to show results at the end of the year to justify their share of their firm's profits. In fact, an outsider to the litigation world would be surprised how often it is possible to settle a case in late December when a plaintiff's lawyer realizes that he needs a quick settlement in order to make his annual budget. In short, the world of human decision-making is far too complicated to be definitively reduced to a model.

Nevertheless, policy makers (like legislators and judges) make policy all the time based upon certain assumptions. In some situations those assumptions are articulated and organized into models. In other situations, the assumptions are tacit or unspoken and yet still vital to the policy-making function. So, while I recognize that any model must be inherently limited because of the complexities of human behavior, the very act of talking about public policy choices requires that I adopt a model, either explicitly or implicitly, and I've chosen to make my choice of a model explicitly.

The Opportunity Curve Model of Disputes

I'll begin with the assumption that most disputes that have the potential to result in civil litigation are fundamentally economic. As assumptions go, I think this one is on fairly safe ground. In a dispute over a contract, the subject matter is primarily economic. One party may want money from the other. One party may want the other to perform some service (which can have an impact measured in economic terms). In most tort cases, the relief sought by the plaintiff is an award for money damages. Whether the plaintiff is seeking compensation for damages suffered or for a perceived impact on future values resulting from the defendant's alleged wrongdoing, the parties measure the lawsuit in dollars.

By using economics as the organizing principle of a decision-making model, however, I am not suggesting that the parties to a dispute have no noneconomic concerns. Noneconomic concerns often motivate plaintiffs in certain areas of policy-related litigation. For example, environmental advocates often sue to try to influence environmental issues, such as the construction of factories, the development of real estate and the use of public lands. Class action litigants sometimes seek injunctive relief, requesting the court to order an industry or a company to refrain from certain behaviors. Other kinds of advocates may sue private parties or the government to try to force certain policy outcomes.

While the proponents of public policy litigation may have non-economic motivations (improving the environment, achieving social justice goals, etc.) their opponents generally have economic goals or have objections that rely on economic justifications. For example, an environmental group that sues a power company over the construction of a nuclear power plant may be motivated by their concerns for the environment, but the power company (while perhaps expressing a shared concern over the environment) will measure its prospects and its success in the dispute in economic terms (i.e., its cost of defense, the money damages it might pay, the cost of the power plant, the new revenues it anticipates from the new power plant, etc.). An industry or private company that is sued over its business practices must consider the cost of changing its practices and the impact on revenue and expense that will result from those changes.

In short, my model claims that each party to a lawsuit perceives a potential future outlay of expenses and a potential future recovery. If that party's perception were graphed, where the net difference between the party's best possible recovery and worst possible outlay of expenditures were set forth on the vertical axis and the time spent in litigation were set forth on the horizontal axis, in nearly every hypothetical case the party would perceive a curve that would begin at its highest point at the very beginning of the dispute and would curve downward and to the right as the litigation took place over time.

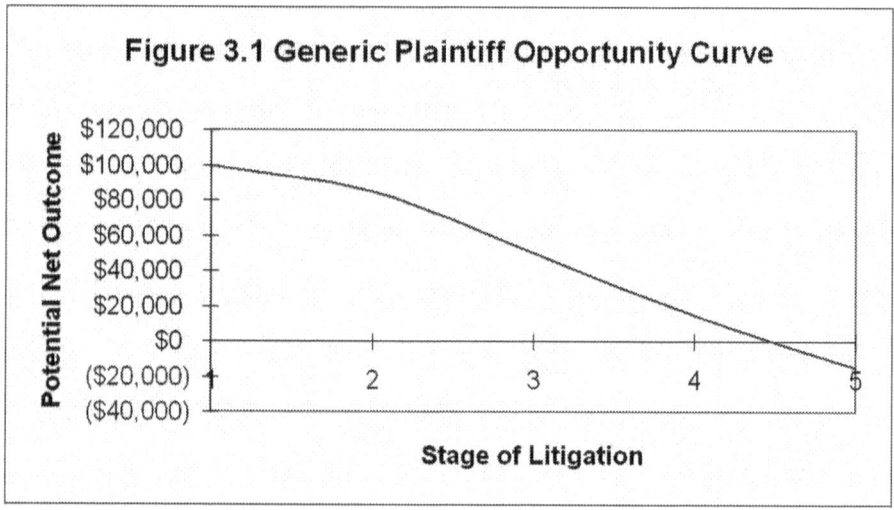

Figure 3.1 Generic Plaintiff Opportunity Curve

Let's explore this in another example. Imagine a contract dispute in which the plaintiff believes it is entitled to $100,000 in payment. The plaintiff consults a lawyer and is told that it would have to pay the following amounts at the following stages of the litigation process: (1) sending a simple letter demanding payment ($5,000); (2) filing the complaint ($10,000); (3) filing the complaint and prevailing on an adverse preliminary motion to dismiss ($25,000), (4), taking discovery and prevailing on a motion for summary judgment ($75,000); and (5) filing the complaint, taking discovery, conducting and winning at trial and pursuing the judgment after trial ($150,000). Assume also that the contract does not allow the plaintiff to recover from the defendant any of its costs or expenses in collecting the amounts due under the contract. In this hypothetical, the plaintiff's decision-making model (proceed or not proceed) would look something like this:

Plaintiff's Decision-Making Model
Table 3.1

Potential Action	Cumulative Cost	Benefit	Net
1. Send demand letter	($5,000)	$100,000	$95,000
2. File complaint	($10,000)	$100,000	$90,000
3. Prevail on preliminary motion	($25,000)	$100,000	$75,000
4. Prevail on summary judgment	($75,000)	$100,000	$25,000
5. File complaint / win at trial / pursue judgment	($150,000)	$100,000	($50,000)

In this hypothetical, the model suggests that the plaintiff would proceed with litigation if it thought it could prevail at the summary judgment stage or earlier (because any of those alternatives would yield a positive net benefit) but would not proceed if it had to go through trial (because in that situation the net benefit would be negative). Moreover, given a choice between prevailing at the preliminary stage of writing a demand letter versus proceeding to litigation, the plaintiff would prefer to prevail before commencing litigation because doing so yields the highest possible net benefit.

Putting this model in graphic form makes the plaintiff's reason for decision even more clear:

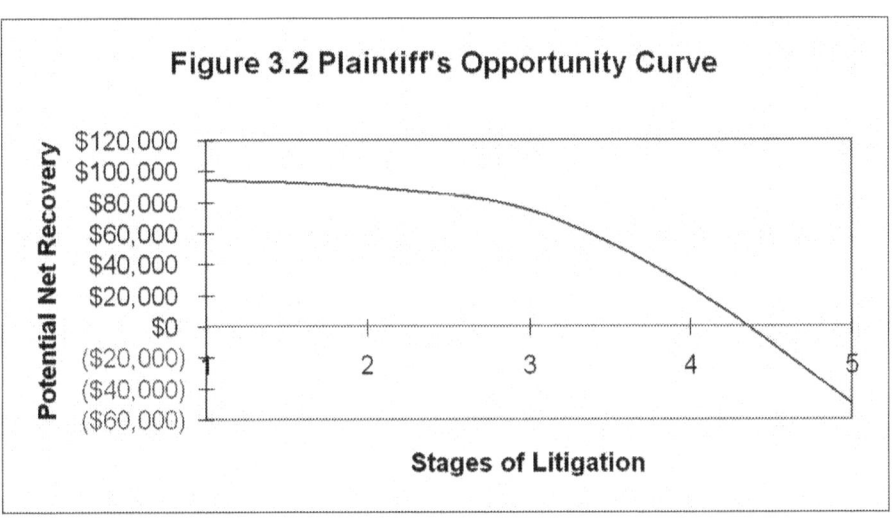

Figure 3.2 Plaintiff's Opportunity Curve

As this graph shows, even from the outset of the dispute the plaintiff can perceive that there is a future point in time at which its net outcome (even assuming a "win" for the full amount claimed in the dispute) is zero or less than zero. The inflection point on the plaintiff's opportunity curve (where its best possible outcome is zero or less than zero) in practical terms is when this dispute becomes no longer "worth it". Acknowledging at the outset that there will come a time when a lawsuit is no longer worthwhile gives the plaintiff an incentive to discount its claim early in the process so that it can realize a net recovery before reaching the point of inflection.

These conclusions should appear to be elementary because they are. That's why this economic model of decision-making is appealing. In the simplest possible hypothetical, the model reaches the obvious outcome for the obvious reasons.

At the same time, we can imagine the decision-making of the defendant. The defendant may truly believe that it is not obligated to pay the plaintiff (perhaps because it believes the services were not delivered in accordance with the contract or because the plaintiff failed to satisfy some other requirement under the contract). Because the defendant is being asked to pay the plaintiff's demand, however, (i.e., the $100,000 that plaintiff contends is due under the contract) the benefit that the defendant hopes to realize is a negative (i.e., avoiding having to pay $100,000).

Imagine that the defendant in this case consults a lawyer, and the lawyer outlines the following options:

a.   the defendant can pay the $100,000 if the plaintiff demands it and owe the lawyer only $5,000 for this initial consultation;

b.   the defendant can refuse to pay on an initial demand letter, but concede and pay the $100,000 only if the plaintiff files a complaint (at which point its attorneys' fees will amount to $10,000);

c.   the defendant can refuse to pay, even after litigation is commenced, but concede and pay $100,000 only if the plaintiff prevails on a summary judgment motion (at which point the defendant's attorneys' fees will be $75,000); or

d.   the defendant can refuse to pay unless it loses at trial (at which point the defendant would owe the $100,000 under the contract plus $150,000 in fees to its attorneys).

In this hypothetical the defendant's net outcome is always negative. Consequently, the defendant will choose the alternative that is the least negative, which would be a quick settlement at the demand stage (when defendant's total outlay would only be $105,000).

Defendant's Decision-Making Model (Table 3.2)			
Potential Action	**Cost**	**Benefit**	**Net**
Demand letter	($5,000)	($100,000)	($105,000)
Complaint	($10,000)	($100,000)	($110,000)
Complaint / summary judgment	($75,000)	($100,000)	($175,000)
Complaint / Trial / Judgment	($150,000)	($100,000)	($250,000)

Comparing the decision-making models of both the plaintiff and defendant illustrate the obvious solution to this dispute:

Combined Plaintiff and Defendant Decision-Making Model (Table 3.3)			
Potential Action	**Plaintiff's Net Outcome**	**Defendant's Net Outcome**	**Total Transaction Costs**
Demand letter	$95,000	($105,000)	$10,000
Complaint	$90,000	($110,000)	$20,000
Complaint / summary judgment	$25,000	($175,000)	$150,000
Complaint / trial / judgment	($50,000)	($250,000)	$300,000

If this situation occurred in reality, where the plaintiff's best outcome was settlement at the demand letter stage and the defendant's best outcome was the same, the parties would almost invariably reach this outcome. Again, the conclusion is elementary, but it demonstrates the validity of this model.

Another conclusion shown by this model is how the outcome to society is more efficient at the earliest stages of the process and less efficient at the later stages. When the case settles at the first stage, the plaintiff recovers $90,000 and the total attorneys' fees for both parties are $10,000. Recalling from Chapter 1 how efficiency compares the value transferred against the value expended in creating that transfer, this outcome is 90% efficient. If the case is resolved at the summary judgment stage such that the plaintiff realizes a net recovery of $25,000 but

the total transaction costs are $150,000, the efficiency outcome is only 14% effi-
cient. If the case had gone to trial, the efficiency outcome would have been even
worse.

These very elementary numbers display a profound truth that is at the heart of
the problem with the U.S. litigation system. Parties to a dispute perceive a range
of potential choices they may exercise but, as the litigation or dispute resolution
process continues over time, the net outcome each party hopes to realize declines
in value. Changes to procedural rules of litigation that encourage the resolution
of disputes more quickly tend to reduce the transactional costs of litigation and
improve the net outcomes for both parties. Rules that discourage the early resolution of disputes (or those that tend to delay resolution) tend to increase transactional costs and degrade the net outcomes for both parties.

In addition to the private outcomes realized by the party, society as a whole
benefits from the expedited resolution of disputes. Rules that encourage litigation
to continue increase inefficiency and the dissipation of society's assets. Rules that
expedite the resolution of disputes improve efficiency and decrease the waste of
society's assets.

Reality, however, is more complicated. Let's assume that the defendant has a
legal argument that, if it prevails, would leave the defendant owing nothing. Let's
assume that, based upon the available information the defendant believes it has a
fifty percent chance of prevailing with this argument. Let's also assume that this
argument is one that can only prevail if it is argued to the fact-finder at a trial on
the merits (and not in a legal argument to the judge on a preliminary motion or a
motion for summary judgment).

Taking these assumptions into account makes the defendant's decision-making model more complicated. At the outset of the dispute the defendant perceives
several alternative courses of action that could be more or less favorable, depending on the likelihood of success. In this hypothetical, it continues to be the defendant's "best" outcome to settle quickly. In a quick settlement, the defendant will
only owe $105,000. On the other hand, the defendant perceives a 50% chance of
owing the plaintiff nothing. Certainly, the defendant would prefer an outcome
where it owes nothing to an outcome where it pays $105,000. Even if it prevails
at trial, however, the defendant will still have paid $150,000 in attorneys' fees. As
a result, a quick settlement for $105,000 remains the defendant's best choice
(assuming there are no other factors involved in the decision).

But, if the dispute does not settle at the demand letter or complaint-filing
stage and if the defendant's perception of a 50% likelihood of owing nothing persists as the litigation progresses, the defendant develops an incentive *not* to settle.

Once the litigation has proceeded up to the summary judgment stage, the defendant faces a choice of (a) settling by paying the plaintiff $100,000 (which, with the defendant's $75,000 in attorneys' fees will leave the defendant with a net loss of $175,000), or (b) proceeding to trial with a 50% likelihood of losing (where the net loss would be a total outlay of $250,000) and a 50% likelihood of winning (where the net loss would consist of the $150,000 in attorneys' fees already incurred). Depending upon the defendant's perception of risk and other factors, a defendant might be willing to wager $25,000 (the difference between the total cost of settlement at summary judgment versus the potential net outcome of winning at trial) against $75,000 (the additional amount the defendant will pay if it declines to settle at summary judgment but eventually loses at trial).

In this case, the defendant's potential dispositive argument gives the defendant some hope that, if it can continue with the litigation process, its net outcome might not be as bad as if it settled the case and paid the full amount of the plaintiff's claims.

Risks and Rewards

The decision-making model becomes much more complicated when we introduce the concept of uncertainty. Uncertainty plays a role in our decision-making every day. If you have a job, you go to work every day with the understanding that at the end of the week you'll get a paycheck. There's always a risk that you won't get paid. For most people, however, that risk is so negligible that they discount it when they make the decision to go to work each day.

Risk works differently in making decisions that have the potential to result in a benefit. You may decide to buy a lottery ticket. A $1 lottery ticket might give you a 1:10 million potential of winning $1 million. A purely economic analysis of buying a lottery ticket where the payoff is $1 million but the odds of winning are 1 in 10 million would suggest that buying the ticket is an economically irrational decision. If you bought one thousand tickets every day for $1,000, you might eventually win the lottery and collect $1 million, but in the long run you would lose more than you would win. Nevertheless, state lotteries in the U.S. raise billions of dollars every year in lottery proceeds and the casinos in Las Vegas generate lots of profits offering consumers the chance to win with odds that are even worse than this. Clearly, people often make decisions involving risk that are economically irrational.

People evaluate risk differently in different contexts as well. In one study an MIT professor compared the likelihood of winning the lottery to the likelihood of getting killed in an airline crash. Whether the listener believed that the likelihood of a fatal airline crash was high or not depended on the language used to compare that likelihood to the chance of winning the lottery. When told that they could buy a lottery ticket on the way to catch a plane and stand a better chance of dying on the flight than winning the lottery, listeners thought air travel was unsafe. When told, "If you took one jet flight a day every day, you would go 33,000 years before succumbing to a fatal crash" they were reassured. Somehow, people perceive risk more favorably when they hope for a favorable result and perceive it less favorably when they hope to avoid an unfavorable result.[35]

In the litigation context, however, uncertainty plays different roles for different parties. A plaintiff who believes it has a 1 in 10 chance of winning $100,000 in damages in a lawsuit will probably want to pursue that claim if the plaintiff perceives that potential benefit to outweigh the costs. The trick in understanding a plaintiff's decision to litigate is in perceiving what level of costs the plaintiff will perceive to be "worth it".

Let's imagine that the plaintiff's claim for $100,000 is not quite as open-and-shut as contemplated above. Let's imagine that the plaintiff consults with an attorney and develops some educated guesses about the likelihood that he will actually recover the full amount of his $100,000 claim as follows:

a.   20% likelihood that the defendant will pay the entire $100,000 claim simply upon receiving a demand letter from an attorney (in which event the plaintiff will still have paid $5,000 in attorneys' fees);

b.   30% likelihood that the defendant will pay the entire $100,000 claim (after ignoring the initial demand letter) after the plaintiff files a complaint (in which event the plaintiff will have paid $10,000 in attorneys' fees);

c.   20% likelihood that the defendant will pay the entire $100,000 claim—whether as a consequence of plaintiff's winning a motion for summary judgment or because defendant is no longer willing to proceed with the litigation (after ignoring the demand letter and fighting through the filing of the complaint), in which event the plaintiff will have paid $75,000 in attorneys fees; and

35.   David Wessel, *Vioxx, Tsunami Present the Puzzle of Risk*, Wall Street Journal Online, *available at* http://online.wsj.com/public/page/,public_home_search, 00.html#SB110496947755818185

d. if the case proceeds to trial, it will be resolved either through: (i) an 80% likelihood that the defendant will lose a trial and pay the entire $100,000, or (ii) a 20% likelihood that the defendant will win at trial and pay the plaintiff $0 (again leaving the plaintiff bearing $150,000 in attorneys' fees).

In this circumstance the plaintiff will perceive its decision-making process very differently than under the previous hypotheticals where the plaintiff had no uncertainty as to the ultimate outcome. In this model, the plaintiff must consider not only his costs, which are 100% certain, but also the possibility of his potential recovery and its likelihood:

Plaintiff's Decision-Making Model
(Table 3.4)

Potential Action	Cost	Benefit	Likelihood	Net
Demand letter—Settlement	($5,000)	$100,000	20%	$95,000
Complaint—Settlement	($10,000)	$100,000	30%	$90,000
Complaint / summary judgment—Settlement or Favorable Ruling	($75,000)	$100,000	20%	$25,000
Complaint / Trial / **Prevail**	($150,000)	$100,000	80%	($50,000)
Complaint / Trial / **Lose**	($150,000)	$0	20%	($150,000)

In this model, the plaintiff's decision-making is more complicated. It is still the plaintiff's first preference to settle quickly, yielding a net benefit of $95,000 if the dispute settles after the demand letter or $90,000 if the defendant concedes after the complaint is filed. After these preliminary stages of the litigation, however, the calculus changes. If the defendant has not settled, the plaintiff is forced to make a hard decision: if it settles at the summary judgment stage, it still yields a positive net outcome, but if the case goes to trial, the defendant *no longer has any chance* of a positive net benefit, the benefit can only be negative. Moreover, if the case goes to trial and the plaintiff loses (recognizing a 20% likelihood of that occurring) the plaintiff's net outcome is a substantial negative amount.

From this perspective, it also becomes clear that the plaintiff has some other choices. The plaintiff might decide to have its attorney send a demand letter just to see whether or not the defendant then settles. If the defendant does, the plaintiff obtains its best-case outcome. If the defendant does not settle, the plaintiff can then decide whether or not to take the next step. If the plaintiff proceeds to file the complaint, the plaintiff can see whether or not the defendant decides to settle at that point. If the defendant settles, the plaintiff realizes its second-best case outcome. If the defendant doesn't settle, the plaintiff can then make the (more difficult) decision on whether to proceed (in which circumstance the best outcome the plaintiff can hope to get is a $25,000 net benefit) or not proceed (in which circumstance the plaintiff will have paid only $10,000 and will forgo a possible net benefit of $25,000, but will avoid the possible $150,000 loss it would realize by going to trial and losing).

This hypothetical also suggests an important understanding about the way the plaintiff will make decisions in this case. At the outset of the dispute, the plaintiff may decide to do nothing, dropping its $100,000 claim, but incurring no costs. If it simply concedes, the plaintiff's net outcome (i.e., the "best worst-case") is $0. The plaintiff's best-case alternative at the outset is a net benefit of $95,000 (i.e., spending $5,000 in costs to recover $100,000 from the defendant). Over time, and as transaction costs mount, however, the plaintiff's best-case alternative (recovering $100,000) eventually becomes less desirable than the plaintiff's best worst-case alternative at the beginning ($0). The period of time preceding the point of inflection is one in which the plaintiff has an opportunity to trade risk (in the form of costs) for potential reward (the recovery). After the point of inflection, however, there is no longer any net reward, as the best-case alternative is still a net loss for the plaintiff.

In the hypotheticals so far we have assumed that the plaintiff will have the sole choice, at each stage in the litigation, either to settle with a compromise on the value of the claim or to proceed with litigation for the full value. If the defendant has a counterclaim, however, the decision-making model changes again.

Let's imagine that the defendant in this case has a counterclaim that it believes is worth $75,000. With the presence of a counterclaim, the model is complicated by the possibility that the plaintiff can prevail on its primary claim (in a best-case scenario), lose its primary claim but prevail on the counterclaim (a middle possibility) or lose on both its primary claim and on the counterclaim (in a worst-case result).

Under these assumptions the plaintiff's decision-making model would look like this:

		Plaintiff's Decision-Making Model			
		(Table 3.5)			
Stage	**Action**	**Cumulative Cost**	**Outcome from Primary Claim**	**Outcome from Counterclaim**	**Net**
Demand letter and Settlement	Proceed—Both	$0	$100,000	$0	$95,000
	Concede—Both		$0	$0	$0
	Proceed—Split		$100,000	($75,000)	$20,000
Complaint and Settlement	Proceed—Both	($5,000)	$100,000	$0	$90,000
	Concede—Both		$0	$0	($5,000)
	Proceed—Split		$100,000	($75,000)	$15,000
Complaint, summary judgment, then Settlement or Favorable Ruling	Proceed—Both	($10,000)	$100,000	$0	$25,000
	Concede—Both		$0	$0	($10,000)
	Proceed—Split		$100,000	($75,000)	($50,000)
Complaint, Trial and Judgment	Proceed—Prevail Both	($75,000)	$100,000	$0	($50,000)
	Proceed—Lose Both		$0	($75,000)	($225,000)
	Proceed—Prevail Split		$100,000	($75,000)	($125,000)
	Concede		$0	$0	($75,000)

With the defendant's $75,000 counterclaim in play, the plaintiff needs to be more careful. Although the plaintiff can still hope for a risk-free settlement and a net benefit of $95,000 under the best-case scenario, the counterclaim makes this outcome less likely. What the plaintiff perceives is a range of possible outcomes. The most optimistic is the quick settlement for the full claim. The worst-case outcome begins at $0 and until the second stage in the litigation the plaintiff retains an ability to concede its case and realize a $0 outcome. Later in the case, though, the plaintiff loses that ability. Once the worst-case line falls below $0, the plaintiff cannot avoid the possibility of losing on the counterclaim. In reality, a plaintiff facing this kind of opportunity curve is relatively unlikely to proceed beyond the initial stages of litigation because doing so puts the plaintiff at risk of having an outcome that is worse that simply conceding the case at the outset.

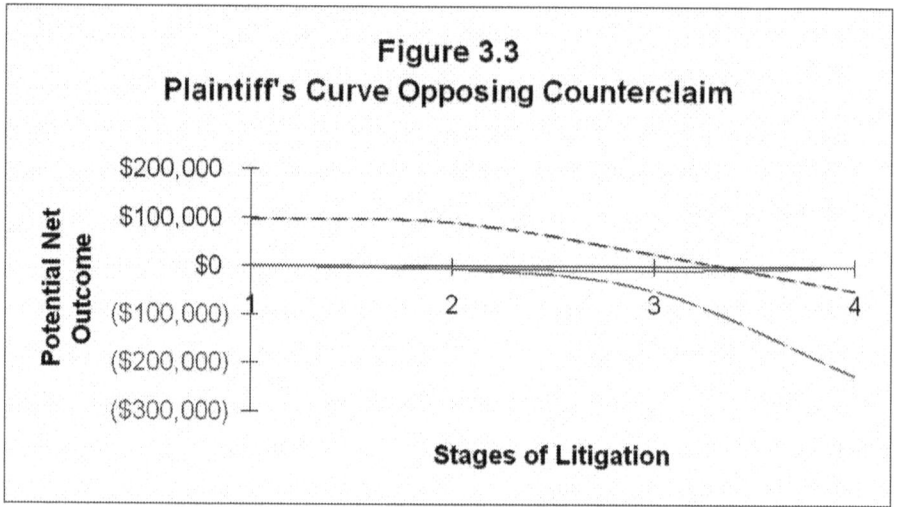

Figure 3.3
Plaintiff's Curve Opposing Counterclaim

The most likely outcome in a case like this is a settlement at an early stage in the litigation where the plaintiff and the defendant compromise by allowing their claims to offset each other, resulting in a payment by the defendant to the plaintiff of less than $100,000. It should also be clear, just from a cursory review of the results that the inflection point on the plaintiff's opportunity curve has moved to the left. As before, this outcome substantiates and quantifies what is intuitively apparent: the presence of a counterclaim puts pressure on the plaintiff to settle and tends to reduce the likelihood of a settlement at the high end of the plaintiff's best-case opportunity curve.

By developing an economic model for understanding litigation decision-making, we can now see how the concept of a declining opportunity curve is critical in creating incentives for both parties to settle their dispute. The more steep the opportunity curve, the greater the urgency for settlement. Also, the sooner the party reaches the inflection point between its opportunity curve and its best worst-case outcome, the greater the urgency for settlement.

These conclusions are not only apparent from the modeling we've done in this chapter, but are also consistent with our intuitive understanding of litigation. In a case where a party is defending against a claim but has a counterclaim of roughly equal value, the party is more likely to think of the two claims as a wash. While the transactional costs of prosecuting the litigation cause the party's opportunity to decline, giving some incentive for early settlement, the party has less urgency than if it had no counterclaim at all. The opposing party (if it values the claims in the same way) will have a similar view. If its claim has no opposing counterclaim, the party perceives a flatter opportunity curve. The presence of a counterclaim steepens the opportunity curve and moves the inflection point to the left. Again, this is entirely intuitive. If you had a claim that was unopposed, you would perceive little value in an early settlement. If your claim was opposed by a counterclaim, you would perceive a greater urgency for settlement.

The hypotheticals I used in describing the economic model assumed that both parties would have to pay attorneys' fees in the same amount. In reality, attorneys' fees can very greatly and, in many cases, plaintiffs don't have to pay attorneys' fees at all.

Contingent Fees

Many of the most aggravating examples of litigation abuse involve cases where the plaintiff's attorneys are working for a contingent fee. In a contingent fee case, the plaintiff pays nothing in cash or up-front for the attorney's time. For his service, the attorney agrees with his plaintiff client that the attorney will get a percentage (a contingent fee) of the plaintiff's recovery (whether that recovery comes from a judgment or from settlement). Contingent fee arrangements can range from a small percentage to as much as 40%. The practice of accepting contingent fees was once quite controversial but is now very familiar in the United States. Elsewhere in the world, however, the practice is less accepted.

How does a contingent fee arrangement affect a plaintiff's opportunity curve and urgency to settle? It flattens the curve, in some situations almost so far that the curve is not a curve at all. The consequence? When the plaintiff has an opportunity curve that is flat, or nearly so, the plaintiff perceives no urgency for settlement. The plaintiff has no incentive to cut short the litigation process (after all, the plaintiff loses nothing but time for as long as the litigation continues) and the plaintiff has no reason to compromise but rather will insist on a full recovery of the plaintiff's entire claim.

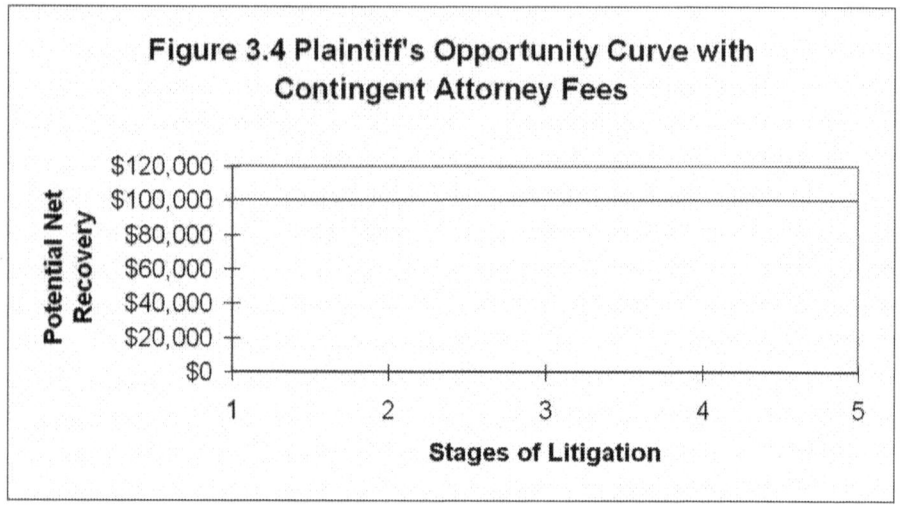

How does a defendant's decision to litigate or settle change when faced with a contingent-fee plaintiff's case? In most situations, the plaintiff's fee arrangement has no impact on the defendant's decision-making. The plaintiff's fee arrangement is confidential and communications between the plaintiff and his attorney are confidential, so the defendant will never know the plaintiff's fee arrangement. But even if the defendant is aware (or suspects) that the plaintiff has a contingent fee arrangement, it is the plaintiff's perception that is sufficient to alter the outcome. So long as the plaintiff perceives no urgency for settlement, the plaintiff will insist on a recovery that is near the high end of the plaintiff's expectations.

Contingent fee arrangements also alter the litigation playing field in a significant way. In the decision-making model so far, we've discussed the plaintiff's perception of settlement urgency as a function of transaction costs. Under a contingent fee arrangement the plaintiff has no transaction costs and no urgency for settlement. The plaintiff's attorney, however, now plays a fundamentally different role. If the plaintiff's attorney is being paid by the plaintiff, in cash, whether on an hourly basis (as nearly all defense attorneys are paid) or on some other basis where the attorney has no stake in the outcome, the attorney has no motivation other than to give the plaintiff good legal advice.

When the plaintiff's attorney gets paid through a recovery, the attorney develops a stake in the litigation and, in a very real sense, develops his own opportunity curve. From the perspective of the plaintiff's attorney, the opportunity curve begins at a high point that is equal to the attorney's contingent fee, taken from the highest possible recovery. Although the plaintiff's attorney will value his time based on the income he could have earned by spending his time on another case, the attorney will still place some value on his time. As the litigation proceeds, the attorney will perceive himself investing more and more of his time into the case. Just like any other party to a dispute, the plaintiff's attorney will perceive a future point of inflection where his opportunity curve will cross his own best worst-case line. The change in the role of the plaintiff's attorney, from legal advisor to stakeholder, is significant.

When the plaintiff's attorney becomes a stakeholder, with a declining opportunity curve, the plaintiff's attorney develops a conflict of interest. That is, an actual conflict of interest (in terms of the attorneys' economic incentives) even if it is not recognized as a conflict of interest for purposes of the law or the attorneys' ethical obligations. Because the plaintiff's attorney doesn't get paid until the litigation settles or until the plaintiff collects an enforceable judgment, the attorney can develop a perspective on the desirability of settlement that might not be the same if the attorney had no personal interest in the outcome. At one extreme, a plaintiff's attorney with a contingent fee may find a temptation to couch his legal advice in terms that encourage his client to settle.

The plaintiff's attorney will only be willing to take on certain kinds of cases on a contingent fee. If the plaintiff's attorney has a choice between taking on a case (getting paid his hourly fee) and taking on a case on a contingent basis, the attorney will compare the amount he could earn on the hourly case versus the potential recovery on the contingent case. To be worth his time, the contingent fee case will have to offer a potential recovery that is at least large enough to equal his anticipated hourly fees.

Some reformers have proposed modifying the rules governing the ability of attorneys to make contingent fee arrangements with their clients. This raises a number of thorny problems, however, as the few rules that do exist are creations of state law and the rules of legal ethics adopted by state bar organizations. Even if there were a magic bullet proposal to regulate how contingent fees worked, there would be no way to implement that proposal without working through both state legislatures and state bar organizations.

The American Rule of Attorneys' Fees

Although we'll discuss this in greater depth in Chapter 4, another feature of the American litigation system that substantially affects the plaintiff's opportunity curve is the American rule of attorneys' fees. In the American system a party may initiate a lawsuit against a defendant, prosecute that case to trial and lose at trial and still have no obligation to reimburse or compensate the defendant for the attorneys' fees it incurred in defending the suit. The American rule stands in contrast to the English rule (which is actually the standard in most countries other than the U.S.) in which the losing party to a lawsuit (whether plaintiff or defendant) is automatically obligated to pay the attorneys' fees of the prevailing party.

The impact of the American rule on the plaintiffs' perceived costs and potential benefit of pursuing a claim in litigation should be obvious. Under the American rule, the slope of the plaintiff's opportunity curve depends solely on the plaintiff's fee arrangement with its attorney. In a contingent fee situation, the plaintiff's opportunity curve is nearly flat and the only urgency for a settlement at less than the perceived full value of the claim comes from the plaintiff's attorney. Under the English rule, even the most optimistic plaintiff must consider the possibility of losing, in which case the defendant's attorneys' fees would become his responsibility. Consequently, a plaintiff's opportunity curve under the English rule will always slope more sharply than under the American rule and reach the inflection point sooner.

While this opportunity curve model may sound theoretical, it is the understanding of how parties perceive incentives to litigate that drives the bulk of the U.S. litigation burden today. By choosing to value the ability of plaintiffs to have their grievances heard in court over the value of defendants to be free from having to pay to defend themselves, Congress and the legislatures have placed a large thumb on the scales of justice. That thumb has imbalanced the system, giving plaintiffs an incentive to sue and an incentive to keep even weak cases in the litigation system because they bear little or no costs. Defendants bear all the costs, in courts chosen by plaintiffs and in the time and manner chosen by plaintiffs. Except for those defendants who can afford to pay to litigate a claim all the way to an uncertain outcome at or near trial, many defendants settle simply to avoid incurring costs. Choosing to keep a system that is out of balance not only hurts the finances of defendants but also imposes massive inefficiencies on society. Society's waste, in terms of money, effort and lost opportunity, increases for every case filed and for every case that persists one day longer than it should. Only a procedural change that removes the incentives for inefficiency can restore the balance, compensating plaintiffs for their actual losses, but reducing the transaction costs that today are borne almost entirely by defendants.

4

The Cost of Litigation is Out of Balance

America's civil justice system is the most expensive in the world.... The threat of frivolous lawsuits has forced many small businesses and doctor's offices to close, leaving countless Americans without meaningful work or access to adequate medical care. Our economy and court system cannot afford the tremendous expense created by these unnecessary proceedings. Small businesses rank the cost and availability of liability insurance as second only to the costs of health care as their top priority. Congressman Tom Cole (4th Dist. Oklahoma). September 27, 2004.

Defendants Bear the Entire Cost of Defense

One of the principles that most often surprises business decision-makers when they become involved in litigation is that the defendant in a lawsuit nearly always bears its entire cost of defense. This fact drives the bulk of the frivolous litigation and accounts for the largest part of the excessive litigation in the U.S. This fact is also an aspect of the American system that makes it almost unique in the world.[36]

As you've seen, it takes very little for a plaintiff to initiate a lawsuit. If the complaint contains the bare minimum legal requirements to "state a claim for which relief can be granted" the complaint will survive preliminary motions to dismiss and the plaintiff will be able to take the defendant through a lengthy and expensive discovery process. Discovery can be long and expensive, especially on the part of the defendant who must produce documents and data at the plaintiff's

---

36. Walter Olson, David Bernstein, *Loser-Pays: Where Next?*, 55 MD. L. REV. 1161 (1996) (discussing how the English rule "appears to be in effect in most if not all jurisdictions outside the United States").

request and make its employees available to give depositions. In addition, before producing documents and giving depositions to the plaintiff, the defendant's attorneys will want to have reviewed those documents and interviewed the relevant witnesses so that they know what facts will come forth in the discovery process. From the point of view of the defense attorney, discovery can consume 50% or more of the entire cost of defending the case.

The commencement of the lawsuit also imposes additional burdens on some defendants. Defendants that are publicly traded (meaning that they have registered their stock through the Securities Exchange Commission and are traded over the NYSE, NASDAQ or one of the other public stock exchanges) have additional disclosure obligations. In determining whether the mere filing of a complaint requires disclosure, the defendant's attorneys must examine both the allegations of the plaintiff and the defendant's likely defenses, analyze the likely outcome or cost of the case, and determine whether all of those considerations (if fully known) would be considered "material" to the view of a "reasonable investor".

In reality this is often not much more than educated guesswork, as the facts of a case are often not fully known when it begins but are teased out over time and through the litigation process. Even when the defendant's attorneys think they do know all of the facts, that doesn't make it much easier to analyze the likely outcome of the case. Attorneys are better at determining what *should* be the proper outcome of a case, rather than predicting what *will* be the actual outcome of a case. As a consequence, attorneys often exercise their powers of prediction conservatively, telling a corporate defendant that the case ought to be resolved in such a manner, but that predicting is imprecise and the case might be resolved in some other manner. This kind of hedging is maddening to corporate officers who must decide whether or not the case should be disclosed and, if so, with what kind of language and description.

If the case is disclosed with too little attention to the plaintiff's allegations and if the plaintiff eventually prevails, the corporation could find itself a defendant again in an action by disgruntled shareholders who will claim that the corporation defrauded them by failing to disclose material information regarding the litigation. On the other hand, if the corporation discloses the case with too much attention and emphasis on the plaintiff's allegations, the market may respond negatively, driving down the value of the corporation's stock. Depressing the stock value immediately impacts all of the corporation's stockholders as well as all of the employees of the company (who often hold stock options that derive their value from the market value of the stock). In short, merely filing a complaint forces a corporate defendant to spend substantial sums on preparing its defense and can destroy millions of dollars in shareholder value merely as a result of the marketplace's perception.

In the fall of 2004, Merck & Co. (NYSE: MRK) was trading at approximately $45 per share. With nearly 2.3 billion shares outstanding, the company had a market capitalization (share price multiplied by number of shares) of nearly $100 billion. With more than 63,000 employees worldwide, Merck generated sales of more than $22 billion per year from its pharmaceuticals, including Propecia™, a drug that addresses male pattern baldness, Singulair™, a treatment for asthma and seasonal allergies, and Vioxx™, an anti-inflammatory drug used to reduce pain, especially in patients with arthritis.

On September 30, 2004, MRK announced that it was voluntarily pulling Vioxx from the market as a result of a study that suggested that sustained use of the drug could increase the risk for heart attacks.[37] The study, which MRK had undertaken itself, was intended to develop data on the possible use of Vioxx for patients with certain types of cancers. When the study developed data that suggested an increase in heart attacks, Vioxx released the news to the public and suspended sales of the drug. The CEO of Merck said in a statement:

> "We are taking this action because we believe it best serves the interests of patients. Although we believe it would have been possible to continue to market VIOXX with labeling that would incorporate these new data, given the availability of alternative therapies, and the questions raised by the data, we concluded that a voluntary withdrawal is the responsible course to take."[38]

At the time the drug was pulled from the market, it had been in distribution for approximately 5 years and was in use in more than 80 countries, generating 2003 worldwide sales of $2.5 billion.

The reaction was immediate and predictable. Within days of the announcement plaintiffs' attorneys filed several lawsuits, including one allegedly on behalf of shareholders claiming that the company engaged in fraud by failing to disclose information known by the company regarding the risks of Vioxx and another allegedly on behalf of Merck employees participating in various retirement funds for supposedly "investing unwisely" in Merck stock. At the same time the U.S.

---

37. Press Release (Sept. 30, 2004) *available at* http://www.vioxx.com/rofecoxib/vioxx/consumer/index.jsp.

38. *Id.*

Food and Drug Administration announced that it would investigate Vioxx as well as some other drugs that relied upon similar chemical processes.

As I write this, in the closing days of December 2004, the full story of Merck and Vioxx remains unknown but some conclusions are obvious. The first is that Merck voluntarily disclosed the potential problems with Vioxx in connection with a study that it initiated and funded for the purpose of developing additional uses for the drug. No crusading plaintiff or undercover investigation unearthed the "smoking gun". Merck told the truth as it learned it. The information on possible adverse effects was a mere byproduct of Merck's study. At the time of this writing, it is still not clear whether there are any adverse effects from Vioxx but only that one study contained some data that suggested there *might* be adverse effects. It may happen that, at some point in the future, additional studies may determine that this initial study was flawed and that there are no adverse effects from Vioxx. In that case Merck may well re-introduce the product to the market. Alternatively, additional studies may reinforce the first study and Vioxx may never be sold again. Today, we just don't know.

Despite the fact that no one today knows exactly whether Vioxx has adverse effects or whether it is a useful drug, numerous lawsuits have been filed against Merck, including suits allegedly on behalf of patients who took the drug, investors who bought stock in Merck and employees whose retirements are based on Merck's stock. While the attorneys who wrote these complaints cannot possibly know all of the facts—or even the fundamental question of whether there is a problem or not with the drug—they have filed lawsuits, tried to locate potential plaintiffs and issued press releases announcing their suits in order to attract additional potential clients.

Rightfully fearing the cost and burden of litigation and the substantial public relations scandal of the recall, investors have sold down the price of Merck stock from $45 prior to the announcement to a low of $25.60 in early November 2004. This diminution in value itself, across a total of 2.2 billion shares of MRK outstanding, yields a loss of value of approximately $44 billion. That $44 billion loss, felt by every investor who owned stock at the $45 price in late September and who still held at the bottom of the market in early November, far exceeded (a) the total gross sales of Vioxx in 2003 (only $2.5 billion) and (b) the estimated settlement costs for the various lawsuits (estimated by some in the $8 to $9 billion range).

At this point, recall in Chapter 1 when we discussed the concept of "deadweight loss" in the calculation of the overall inefficiency of the litigation process. That loss, which the Council of Economic Advisors estimated in the range of $50 billion per year, included losses resulting from products that would never be launched, and valuable services that would never be offered, out of a fear of litigation. The $44 billion decline in market value suffered by the investors in Merck is not included in the concept of deadweight loss. In this particular case, while the Merck example may be extraordinary and looks to be a substantial story in 2005, the $44 billion loss in Merck's market capitalization almost swamps the $50 billion annual estimate for deadweight loss through the entire U.S. economy.

Is Merck's experience unusual? One popular investment Web site, The Motley Fool™, carried an article—written before the Merck/Vioxx announcement—that concluded that strategic class actions in the biotech market were all too familiar.[39] The article stated that the author had examined the SEC filings of 100 publicly traded biotech companies. Of those 100, 21 were currently defending class action lawsuits surrounding an alleged problem with a drug.

> "I'll admit that when I started this project I suspected many of these suits were frivolous attempts by class action vultures to cash in on a company's misfortune. Drug development is a high-risk business model, where investigational products frequently fail. Approximately 30% of drugs in phase 3 trials will never gain approval, and roughly 20% of drugs filed for approval with the FDA will get turned down. That's a pretty high failure rate.
>
> A skeptic such as myself may think that all a class action firm needs to do to find a potentially lucrative case is to scan these failures for corresponding declines in stock price and look for prior statements from management that were optimistic about the drug's chances. A law firm could put that together and build the argument that management's false statements artificially inflated the market price of the securities, and then hope for a win. How many times does a firm have to be successful to offset the costs of suits that were dismissed or unsuccessful?
>
> This opinion is reinforced after seeing that 21 out of 100 companies are currently facing suits after a drug setback. To me, it is common sense that such a large percentage of companies are not really doing anything wrong. Perhaps some are, but I think a lot of them fall into a gray area concerning whether or not certain statements by management were misleading. I don't place the blame solely on management, though. Often these stocks are inflated by investors hoping a drug works and that they'll hit a big payday. It's not always management's fault when the company's stock gets run up by optimists or momentum traders."

---

39. Charly Travers, *Drug Fails, Get Sued* (July 19, 2004) *available at* http://www.fool.com/news/commentary/2004/commentary04071901.htm.

While this was not an academic study and the author's research was not published with the article, if it's true that 21 out of 100 publicly-traded biotech stocks at any given time are facing a class action lawsuit surrounding a drug they sell (or sold) some conclusions are inescapable. Either 20% of new drugs sold on the market are so dangerous that they spawn massive litigation or there is something inherent in the litigation process that makes these suits profitable for the attorneys who pursue them, regardless of the merits.

While I have no special expertise in the drug industry, I am well acquainted with the tactics of plaintiffs' attorneys who try to leverage the public relations impact of their lawsuits to gain money in settlement. It is not unheard of to have a prospective plaintiffs' attorney contact a corporate defendant—sometimes with a draft of the complaint—to suggest a settlement even before the complaint is filed, banking on the hopes that corporate decision-makers will recognize the potential loss of market capitalization and pay the plaintiff something less than that potential loss simply to avoid it. Needless to say, settlements in such circumstances have nothing to do with the merits of the case and nothing to do with the damage that may have been suffered by the plaintiff. Such settlements are solely a function of a fear of litigation and the avoidance of its huge transaction costs.

The Problem of Class Actions

Class action litigation has also been a significant source of inefficiency. Through the class action rules, plaintiffs' lawyers are able to manufacture supposed "classes" of plaintiffs who have suffered a common injury from the same defendant or group of defendants. The plaintiffs might consist, for example, of customers of a video rental store who paid late fees, customers of an airline who received frequent flyer miles or customers of an electronics manufacturer who all bought the same device. In many instances, the potential plaintiffs have not suffered any significant "injury" at all. The damage may have been purely theoretical or may have been so inconsequential (perhaps a few dollars for each individual) that no reasonable individual plaintiff would have given it a moment's notice. The plaintiffs might all have bought a device on the basis of supposedly "misleading" advertising even though the device functions just fine in ordinary use and few of the customers have complained.

By massing together a large number of similar potential plaintiffs—even if they have no significant injury—the plaintiffs' lawyers can threaten the defendant with the potential of time-consuming and expensive litigation. Under the aegis of this threat, some defendants will settle, giving the plaintiffs coupons for additional purchases, or perhaps a small refund of their actual purchase price, but will be required to pay the plaintiffs' attorneys substantial fees in cash.

This phenomenon has been continuing for several years and has recently begun to attract headlines. One law professor estimated that class action filings in federal courts have increased by 300 percent over the past ten years while filings in state courts have increased by as much as 1,000 percent.[40]

In the now-notorious *Bank of Boston* case, plaintiffs' lawyers assembled a class of customers of the Bank of Boston, claiming that the bank had over-collected money in the customers' home mortgage escrow accounts, profiting by the extra interest earned on the excess collections.[41] The settlement, approved by an Alabama state court, gave each member of the class $8.76 but awarded the class attorneys more than $8.5 million in fees.[42]

Another group of plaintiffs' lawyers sued video rental chain Blockbuster under the theory that the store's late fees were excessive. In settling the case, Blockbuster agreed to give class members coupons for a $1 discount off a future video rental but was forced to pay the plaintiffs' lawyers $9.25 million.[43]

In a class action lawsuit against American Airlines, plaintiffs' lawyers claimed that the airline's frequent flyer program was misleading and deceptive. The airline agreed to settle the suit by giving class members vouchers for a $25-75 discount on future ticket purchases but paid the plaintiffs' lawyers $25 million in attorneys' fees.[44]

While these are only a few examples, they are far from isolated. Class action lawsuits for minor inconvenience-type injuries have become common and are simply a vehicle for plaintiffs' lawyers to generate fees to be paid by deep pocket corporate defendants. A study by the Rand Institute for Civil Justice concluded that the problem was substantial:

> Most consumer class members have only a small financial stake in the litigation. And, because of the way the class action rules are commonly applied, the class members may not even learn of the litigation until it is almost over. Even representative plaintiffs (i.e., those in whose name the suit is filed) may play little role in the litigation. As a result, there are few if any consumer class members who actively monitor the class action attorney's behavior. Such "cli-

---

40. Senate Report 108-123 (July 31, 2003) at 14.
41. *Kamilewicz v. Bank of Boston*, 92 F.3d 506 (7th Cir. 1996).
42. Senate Report 108-123, *supra* n40 at 15.
43. *Id.* at 16.
44. *American Airlines Settles Lawsuits over Frequent Flier Program*, Fort Worth Star-Telegram, June 22, 2000. *See also* Senate Report 108-123, *supra* n40 at 16.

entless" litigation holds within itself the seeds for questionable practices. The powerful financial incentives that drive plaintiff attorneys to assume the risk of litigation intersect with powerful interests on the defense side in settling litigation as early and as cheaply as possible with the least publicity.[45]

The Rand study concluded that this process failed to address effectively the actual injury (if any) done to the consumer, unfairly created a windfall for plaintiffs' attorneys and harmed society through the imposition of unwarranted costs:

> These incentives can produce settlements that are arrived at without adequate investigation of facts and law and that create little value for class members or society. For class counsel, the rewards are fees disproportionate to the effort they actually invested in the case. For defendants, the rewards are a less-expensive settlement than they may have anticipated, given the merits of the case, and the ability to get back to business rather than engage in continued litigation. For society, however, there are substantial costs: lost opportunities for deterrence (if class counsel settled too quickly and too cheaply), wasted resources (if defendants settled simply to get rid of the lawsuit at an attractive price, rather than because the case was meritorious), and—over the long run—increasing amounts of frivolous litigation as the attraction of such lawsuits becomes apparent to an ever-increasing number of plaintiff lawyers.[46]

The rise of mass consumer class actions has also focused attention on those state court jurisdictions that have proven friendly to these claims and the incestuous settlements they induce. Madison County, Illinois, in particular, has gained notoriety.[47] This rural county is home to less than one percent of the U.S. population but had two class action filings in 1998, growing to 39 cases in 2000. The number of class actions in Madison County state courts continued to grow in 2001 and 2002.[48]

Some critics have charged that state jurisdictions that spawn such incredible amounts of class action suits are the result of collusion between wealthy plaintiffs' attorneys and the elected judges sponsored by those attorneys through campaign contributions.[49] One critical assessment of the Madison County situation indi-

---

45.   Deborah R. Hensler et al., *Class Action Dilemmas: Pursuing Public Goals for Private Gain* (Executive Summary) (Rand Institute for Civil Justice) (1999) 9-10.

46.   *Id.* at 10

47.   Critics have called the state courts in Madison County "plaintiff's paradise" and the "lawsuit capital of the world". American Tort Reform Association, *Justice for Sale II* (July 2004) *available at* http://www.atra.org/files.cgi/7814_JusticeForSale-II.pdf.

48.   Senate Report 108-123, *supra* n40 at 14.

cated that judges were receiving up to 90% of their campaign contributions from plaintiffs' attorneys, including, in some instances, attorneys who were appearing before those judges in active cases.[50] Even if such charges are discounted or dismissed, however, the financial incentives for this kind of speculative litigation are clear and the costs are unmistakable.

As the Rand study concluded, the use of class litigation as an indirect method of law enforcement is problematic. Society values the enforcement of its laws but it entrusts law enforcement to the government so that it is subject to political and legal control. Governmental prosecutors exercise discretion, subject to legal controls over that discretion, and have the responsibility for how they enforce laws. Prosecutors determine which cases are "worth it" and which ones aren't. Prosecutors have constraints over their handling of cases and, in general, have no incentive to litigate cases that aren't worth it. Private litigants, in the form of plaintiffs' attorneys, have no similar constraints. To the extent that the system creates economic incentives for plaintiffs' attorneys to enforce laws in situations where governmental prosecutors would abstain from enforcement, the system is rewarding behavior that should be discouraged.

The difficulty with tackling the problem of speculative class action suits, however, is in crafting the solution. The Rand study that assessed the problem concluded that there was no effective solution, other than to encourage judges to scrutinize class action settlements more carefully and with a more critical eye.[51] While the role of judges is important and increased judicial scrutiny would certainly improve the situation, it is impossible to legislate judicial scrutiny. Ultimately, the judges themselves will be the ones to enforce and interpret, using their own sense of priorities, even the boldest law with the most precise instructions. The views of judges will never be uniform and variations in judges' views over these kinds of cases will produce inconsistent results, continuing the incentives for initiating these cases.

The American Rule

The American rule, in which each party to a lawsuit bears its own costs, is truly unique to the American system.[52] In most other jurisdictions, especially those

---

49. *Justice for Sale II, supra* n47.
50. *Id.*
51. *Class Action Dilemmas, supra* n45 at 31.
52. Olson and Bernstein, *Loser-Pays, supra* n36 at 1161.

that follow the English common law as the U.S. does, the loser in a lawsuit pays the attorneys' fees of the winner.[53] While the many variations in legal procedure and the other legal and societal factors that play a role in litigation make it diffi-cult to compare the American and English legal systems,[54] one author has con-cluded that American tort costs are ten times as high per capita as tort costs in England.[55]

Although the concept of a loser-pays rule for shifting the burden of attorneys' fees is generally called the "English rule" it is actually the standard in almost every legal system in the world other than in the U.S. While there are a myriad of legal and social factors that contribute to the frequency and cost of litigation, it is per-haps this factor above all others than makes the cost of litigation in the U.S., as a percentage of GDP, the highest in the world.[56]

The purpose of the English rule is three-fold. First, it deters parties from initi-ating lawsuits that have a low likelihood of success but a high payout in the event of a fluke victory. Second, it dissuades persons from initiating lawsuits that have little chance of success in hopes of extracting a settlement payment from a defen-dant who wants to avoid the costs of litigation. Third, it encourages parties who are defending against meritorious claims to settle those cases quickly, giving them an incentive to make the resolution of the matter as efficient as possible.[57]

A number of reformers, including Professor David Bernstein and Walter Olson of the Manhattan Institute, have suggested adopting the English rule as a solution for the problem of excessive litigation. We'll explore this notion as well as some related concepts in Chapter 7. Even if adopting the English rule is not the solution to the problem, however, the American rule itself is a big part of the problem.

The American rule, simply put, gives the plaintiff a "free shot" at the defen-dant. The best rationale for the American rule is that it allows equal access to the

---

53. David E. Bernstein, *Procedural Tort Reform: Lessons from Other Nations*, REGULATION, Vol. 19 (1996).

54. For example, differences that could affect the cost of litigation in the American sys-tem in contrast to the English system include variations in per capita income, the availability of social welfare programs to offset the loss of income suffered as a result of injury, the varying roles of juries and judges in the two systems, the availability of insurance and the availability of non-litigation alternatives for recovering damages.

55. P.S. Atiyah, *Tort Law and the Alternatives: Some Anglo-American Comparisons*, 1987 DUKE L.J. 1002, 1012.

56. Tillinghast-Towers Perrin, *supra* n7.

57. *Id.*

courts for all, with even the least powerful consumer having the power to compel the largest corporation into court. The problem, as always, is one of balance. If any individual can compel anyone else (both individuals and corporations) to hire an attorney in self-defense, then all of society is constrained by its most litigious members. If everyone is free to sue, then everyone is capable of being sued and all of society must bear the costs incurred by those who insist on litigation.

In a speculative suit, a plaintiff with a claim that is unlikely to prevail but would have a massive payoff if it did win gets a free ticket to a lottery through the American rule. Knowing that it is unlikely to have to reimburse the defendant or bear any other sanction, a creative plaintiffs' attorney who can develop a long shot theory has every incentive to give it a try. The defendant will acknowledge that it has little chance of recouping its fees and will be forced to settle with the plaintiff, usually working a discount backwards from the plaintiff's best-case scenario outcome.

Speculative lawsuits often take shape as class actions because the class action vehicle lets plaintiffs' attorneys bring together large numbers of potential plaintiffs in a single group. Much of the American class action rules involve the "opt-out" feature, where persons who might theoretically be part of the class are counted as taking part in the case (usually without their knowledge) unless they affirmatively decide to "opt-out" of the litigation through a court-approved notice procedure.

In the realm of high-value mass tort cases, this calculus of risk and reward virtually guarantees that every announcement of potentially adverse news to a corporate defendant will be accompanied by at least one high-publicity case, either on behalf of ostensibly aggrieved customers or shareholders. The litigation will serve little societal benefit, but will divert massive amounts of funds from companies and their investors in favor of those few plaintiffs who participate in the plaintiffs' class and (even more so) the attorneys who initiate the litigation.

The second way that the American rule creates incentives for weak cases is through the "impositional" suit. This variety involves a weak claim in which the plaintiff will recover very little even if it prevails. Nevertheless, because defending the suit allows the plaintiff to impose the cost of defense on the defendant, it gives the plaintiff leverage to negotiate. Although the plaintiff will usually bluff as if it intends to litigate the case to trial, the plaintiff generally begins settlement negotiations with a view towards extracting from the defendant an amount that is only slightly less than what it would cost the defendant to defend the case to the end. In the words of one federal judge, the American rule does "*not* make prevailing parties truly whole by saddling their adversaries with the winners' legal expenses."[58]

Learning how litigation actually works in this country often surprises businesspersons who haven't had experience in U.S. courts. "They can't do that; can they?" is the cry. Unfortunately, the answer is "yes, they can and they do."

Rewarding Ignorance

The American rule creates two additional perverse incentives that create inefficiency. The first is that the incentive to litigate actually tends to reward those plaintiffs (and their counsel) who are less able to acknowledge the strengths and weaknesses of their case.

One of the phenomena I have seen time and time again is where a potential plaintiff (perhaps an aggrieved customer) writes or calls the corporate defendant to raise a complaint. Perhaps the customer thinks the product was defective or the service was poor. The corporate defendant, usually through its customer service employees, talks the customer through a maze of explanations. The customer service department might describe why the product wasn't defective, why the service wasn't poor, might offer a refund or a service credit, and might even apologize in an attempt to mollify the customer and preserve the possibility of a future customer relationship. Failing that, the customer service department at least wants to resolve the issue so that it doesn't find its way into litigation.

At some later time, however, if the customer wasn't satisfied, the customer enlists the aid of an attorney, who then writes a letter to the company setting forth the customer's concerns. In the usual format, the customer's attorney will begin the litany of complaints with the preface "it is my understanding that...." to signal that his understanding of the facts is based on what his client told him. With that beginning, the customer's attorney will list the customer's complaints and then outline how these concerns could add up to a cause of action against the company.

As an attorney who has handled hundreds of letters just like this, let me tell you what all in-house attorneys hope for in this context: that the plaintiff's attorney will be smart enough to know why litigation ultimately is a losing strategy. In most companies there is a form letter for use in these circumstances—not because anyone wants to read a form letter but because this circumstance is repeated so

---

58. *Zapata Hermanos Sucesores, S.A. v. Hearthside Baking Co., Inc.*, 2001 WL 1000927 (N.D. Ill. 2001) (Shadur, J.).

often that it doesn't make sense to "re-invent the wheel" every time it happens. The company's response to the customer's lawyer will set out all of the company's arguments, sometimes even giving away information that is unknown to the customer, in the hopes that the company can educate the customer's lawyer to the view that litigation is a losing strategy.

If the company has a contract that it uses with its customers, the company will provide the lawyer with a copy. The letter will outline all of the major defenses, which will usually include: (a) contractual limitations on the ability of the customer to sue, (b) contractual limitations on the kinds of damages a customer may recover from the company, and (c) contractual limitations on the amount of damages a customer may recover. Although such contractual limitations sometimes require some effort to be enforced in the courts, they are generally enforceable and will usually derail a determined customer's attempts to recover substantial sums from a corporate defendant in a case involving a defective product or service.

Even more importantly, if the company has this kind of information available, the company will often disclose to the customer's lawyer facts that the customer might not otherwise know: the kinds of facts that would come out during the discovery process but might not be publicly available. As before, the purpose of doing this is to educate the customer's attorney towards the view that a fully litigated case on the customer's claims will not yield much, if anything.

Finally, near the end, the letter will state that, although the company is confident that it would prevail if the case were litigated, nevertheless as an offer of compromise and settlement the company is willing to pay a specified amount for a full release of all claims. If the plaintiff's attorney is smart—and assuming that the company has been truthful in its disclosures and is correct in its assessment of the legal merits of the case—the plaintiff (for that is what the customer has effectively become by this point) will take this initial offer or something close to it. While the customer may have no legally-cognizable claim or may have a claim that is worth very little, the company will often make an offer that is enough to give the plaintiff/customer some feeling of satisfaction for an amount that is less than what the corporate defendant would have to pay in the initial stages of responding to a filed complaint. For her troubles, the plaintiffs' attorney—who by this point has done little beyond having a conversation with her client and writing a single letter—may (depending on the fee agreement with her client) pocket her hourly rate or else a percentage of the recovery from the company.

The worse outcome, from the perspective of the corporate defendant, however, is where the plaintiff is emotionally engaged to the point of irrationality, having a guttural, angry need to "make the company bleed" through litigation.[59] An even worse outcome is where an emotionally irrational plaintiff is coupled with an attorney who lacks the legal ability to recognize the drawbacks of his case. In that situation, the litigation system works its most perverse outcomes. The defendant may try to dismiss the case through a preliminary motion. If that fails, the parties will proceed through discovery, spending substantial sums but ultimately uncovering nothing that completes the plaintiff's case. The case will eventually resolve in favor of the defense—either at summary judgment or at trial—but with a net result of nothing in favor of the plaintiff. The defense, of course, will have spent tens or even hundreds of thousands of dollars all to prove to the plaintiff and his lawyer that they were entitled to nothing. Consequently, those plaintiffs and their lawyers who are less able to understand the weaknesses of their own case will require defendants to spend more to extricate themselves from those weak cases.

A second perverse incentive under the American rule is that a defendant involved in a case that it believes is truly merit-worthy (i.e., one that it thinks it will lose) may find that stalling the case is a better outcome than simply settling and paying. In those cases where the plaintiff's real damages are modest—and there is no hope for punitive damages or some other kind of windfall recovery—the plaintiff will usually perceive a value in settling the case quickly. Except for those statutes that allow a plaintiff to earn pre-judgment interest, a plaintiff's expected damages don't ordinarily include a factor that accounts for the time and effort it took for the plaintiff to secure its recovery. By stalling, or at least creating the impression that the defendant will drag out the litigation process, the defendant can use the cost of litigation as leverage against the plaintiff, driving down the plaintiff's price of settlement.

I mention this as a "perverse" effect of the American rule because it is usually the pro-plaintiff groups that oppose any suggestion of adopting the English rule. While two of the three purposes cited above for the English rule relate to deterring weak claims, the third is that the English rule would actually encourage the speedy settlement of strong claims because of the defendant's incentive to minimize the costs of both parties. Thus, the English rule of attorney fee-shifting pro-

---

59. I am aware of one case involving a putative class action by a former employee where the former employee had circulated e-mails to current employees of the company, asking those employees to join him in a class action against the company, promising that he would "make [the company] bleed" through litigation. While this particular individual had little formal education, he knew enough to try to use the company's legal expense as leverage to extract a settlement in his favor.

motes efficiency in both directions, by deterring weak cases and promoting the early settlement of strong cases.

Permitting Irresponsibility

At this point, the opponents of reform will often argue that current statutes already exist to punish parties and their attorneys for pursuing frivolous litigation. While there are frivolous litigation statutes on the books, these tools simply do not do enough to change the basic calculus of litigation and that is why excessive litigation continues to cost us more than $280 billion every year.

Sanctions Against Parties

Most states have a statute that prohibits "frivolous" or "vexatious" litigation. In my home state of Georgia, for example, the key statute is Official Code of Georgia Annotated Section 9-15-14. That statute provides, in part, that "attorney's fees and expenses of litigation shall be awarded to any party against whom another party has asserted a claim…with respect to which there existed such a complete absence of any justiciable issue of law or fact that it could not be reasonably believed that the court would have accepted the asserted claim…." A later provision of the statute also provides that "the court may assess reasonable and necessary attorney's fees and expenses of litigation in any civil action in any court of record if…it finds that an attorney or party brought or defended an action…that lacked substantial justification…." While this statute applies only to cases filed in Georgia courts, it is not very different from similar statutes in many other states.

In practice, however, it is very difficult for defendants to recover their attorneys' fees under this provision. First, it is not enough for the defendant simply to "win" the case. The defendant must dispose of the case either at summary judgment or at the preliminary motion stages. Since the standard at these stages of litigation is very low (i.e., that the complaint merely "states a claim on which relief can be granted" or that the evidence is sufficient for a reasonable fact-finder to rule in favor of the plaintiff) it is easy for a very weak case to survive until the trial stage, at which point the defendant cannot hope to have recourse through the statute. Second, while it is a necessary prerequisite that the defendant prevails at summary judgment in order to use this statute to recover its fees, prevailing is not sufficient. After prevailing, the defendant must prepare a motion, usually accompanied by a memorandum of law that marshals the applicable arguments, for filing with the court. When the court determines to hear the motion, the defendant bears the burden of persuading the court that the plaintiff's claim had "a complete absence of any justiciable issue of law or fact" or "lacked substantial justification."

As a practical matter, this is a difficult burden to carry. Judges are usually happy to clear cases off their dockets and often don't wish to be troubled with debates about the merits of cases they just dismissed. The law doesn't force judges to consider the circumstances of the recently dismissed case and if the judge is simply not inclined to visit the issue, the defendant's motion can be met with a swift denial. Even if the judge does devote time and attention to the motion, the standard to recover fees is very high. Even an extremely weak or frivolous case might not have "a complete absence" of potentially relevant facts or legal issues. In practice, if a plaintiff's attorney can demonstrate even a fairly speculative or remote theory under which the plaintiff might have recovered, the plaintiff will be able to escape the duty to reimburse the defendant.

Finally, even if the defendant can surmount the high hurdles required to get an award of attorneys' fees, the statute specifically limits the award to "attorneys' fees or expenses of litigation…[that do] not exceed amounts which are reasonable and necessary for defending or asserting the rights of a party." So, even if the court is persuaded that the plaintiff had no legal right to pursue its lawsuit, the court may award the winning defendant less than his entire cost of defense if the court believes that the defendant was less than completely efficient in its defense or that its lawyers were simply too expensive.

Moreover, judges often find themselves having sympathy for a losing plaintiff. The plaintiff may have suffered real injuries, even if the defendant had no responsibility for them. Even if the plaintiff made a misguided attempt to recover money from the defendant, judges can sometimes not help but let their sympathies hold them back from shifting the defendant's cost onto the plaintiff.

While defendants no doubt prefer that statutes exist for the recover of attorneys' fees, in practice those statutes are simply not effective at deterring weak or frivolous cases.

Sanctions Against Attorneys

Opponents of litigation reform will also argue that sanctions exist against plaintiffs' attorneys themselves when they pursue frivolous litigation.

In 1983 Congress modified Rule 11 of the Federal Rules of Civil Procedure to give federal judges greater leeway to penalize parties and their attorneys for making frivolous or unwarranted claims and arguments. Under the 1983 version of Rule 11, the court could sanction a party or its attorney for submitting any pleading in a case in federal court that was not supported by the law or by a "good faith argument for the extension, modification or reversal of existing law." If the court found that a party had violated Rule 11, the court could order that party to reimburse the opposing party's attorneys' fees in responding to the unwarranted pleadings or arguments. The notes of the Advisory Committee to the 1983 amendment made clear that its purpose was to discourage and deter frivolous arguments and to compensate the parties who were harmed by these abuses. The notes of the Advisory Committee claimed that:

> "Experience shows that in practice [pre-1983] Rule 11 has not been effective in deterring abuses.... The new language is intended to reduce the reluctance of courts to impose sanctions,...by emphasizing the responsibilities of the attorney and reinforcing those obligations by the imposition of sanctions. The amended rule attempts to deal with the problem by building upon and expanding the equitable doctrine permitting the court to award expenses, including attorneys' fees, to a litigant whose opponent acts in bad faith in instituting or conducting litigation. Greater attention by the district courts to pleading and motion abuses and the imposition of sanctions when appropriate, should discourage dilatory or abusive tactics and help to streamline the litigation process by lessening frivolous claims or defenses."[60]

Importantly, although the 1983 version of Rule 11 could require a party to reimburse an opposing party's attorneys' fees, that sanction could also be imposed on the attorney who filed unsupported claims or pleadings. By raising the specter of personal liability for attorneys, the rule sharply focused the attention of attorneys on the need to ensure that their arguments were duly supported by the law.

In 1993, however, Congress significantly relaxed Rule 11, making the imposition of sanctions a matter of the court's discretion (and not mandatory), providing that sanctions would ordinarily be paid to the court (and not as reimbursement to the opposing party) and broadening the scope of argument that was permitted, by allowing attorneys to make arguments based upon both existing law, a "nonfrivolous" argument for a change in existing law "or the establishment of new law". This amendment also limited the court's ability to award attorneys' fees to the victims of frivolous claims, providing the court could do so only when the prevailing party specifically sought its fees through a motion. This amendment significantly reduced the effectiveness of Rule 11 as a mechanism for attorney fee reimbursement. In addition, by expanding the range of permitted

---

60.   Fed. R. Civ. P. 11 (Notes of the Advisory Committee to the 1983 Amendment).

arguments to include those for the "establishment of new law" the amendment had the practical effective of permitting parties to try out novel or experimental theories so long as they couched those arguments in the context of "establishing" new law. Obviously, this concept opens the door to any party who wants to establish new law through a novel theory, freeing that party from the fear of sanction so long as the party is frank in describing its arguments as novel.

In 2004, Congress considered possible amendments to Rule 11 that would have reinstated some of the provisions of the 1983 rule in addition to other reforms.[61] The legislation passed the House but died in the Senate. While the legislative interest in Rule 11 is encouraging, it is not clear that Rule 11, even if effectively amended would serve well as a means for compensating the victims of frivolous litigation.

Although Rule 11 applies only to cases that are pursued in federal courts, many states have adopted counterpart versions of Rule 11 that are more or less the same. Like the "vexatious litigation" statutes that allow for recovery against a losing plaintiff, however, both federal Rule 11 and its state analogs today are ineffective in deterring frivolous litigation. Like those other statutes, to recover attorneys' fees under Rule 11 the defendant must prevail at the preliminary motion or summary judgment stage of the case. A case that is fatally weak but that survives through the preliminary stages of the litigation process only to lose at trial will not qualify for possible sanctions. Moreover, to preserve a claim under Rule 11, the defendant must have given notice of the potential violation to the plaintiff's attorney, usually in the form of a letter. The letter acts as the starting point for the calculation of the defendant's attorneys' fees, with the plaintiff's attorney having no responsibility for attorneys' fees prior to the time of notice.

In addition, just as with the vexatious litigation statutes, a winning defendant can make a motion under Rule 11 only at the conclusion of the case, after the defendant has spent substantial sums on fighting and winning and the court is glad to be rid of the case. By this point, however, the defendant has already suffered damage. Many judges are unwilling to extend proceedings under a case that has been concluded due to the "satellite litigation" that is involved in sanctioning a party under Rule 11. A judge that simply doesn't think the sanctions are worth the effort, in his discretion, needn't consider the matter. Of course, even if the defendant's motion is successful in rousing the ire of the judge, there is no guarantee that the court will require the plaintiff's attorneys to reimburse the defen-

---

61. *See* discussion of Lawsuit Abuse Reduction Act in Chapter 10.

dant entirely. The award of sanctions (which can be appealed by the plaintiff's attorneys) can be limited to any amount that the court finds just and proper.

While academics might debate the overall value of recovery statutes and Rule 11 on deterring frivolous litigation, the practical experience of attorneys who manage cases is that these rules can be only marginally helpful. Experienced plaintiffs' attorneys know that they can leverage the enormous cost of litigation to drive a defendant to settle at a lower rate if the case ceases to look promising. If the case settles, the defendant gives up any ability to seek recovery from the plaintiff or its attorneys. Rule 11 and the vexatious litigation statutes are perceived as distant and ineffective. A plaintiff or his attorney who is willing to file a complaint on shaky grounds, hoping to recover $1 million, always counts on the ability to offer a discounted settlement (say, $100,000) if the prospects of success grow dim. The corporate defendant might then reason that its cost of litigating the case to a zero recovery outcome can be several times this amount, making it reasonable to pay $100,000 on a case that is worth nothing (and where the plaintiff's attorneys may have violated Rule 11) to avoid the marginal risk of continuing the fight.[62]

The American rule saves its most perverse effects for those attorneys least able to appreciate the strength of their claims. To the extent that Rule 11 and similar rules have a deterrent effect, that effect is felt most strongly by those attorneys who are more educated and better able to appreciate the weaknesses in their own arguments. Lesser skilled attorneys or those who are blinded by an emotional commitment to their case are less able to perceive their own risk and, consequently, are less deterred. The outcome is a system that rewards those plaintiffs who understand least the problems with their own cases.

If the goal of litigation reform is to reduce the number of cases filed and the cost of the cases that do get filed, it must have as its object changes to the procedure of litigation that discourages meritless cases from being filed and that encourages settlement on reasonable terms at the earliest possible stage in the case. By acting at the very end of the litigation process, Rule 11 and the other currently available schemes for shifting attorneys' fees are simply too remote and

---

62.   In such settlements it is fairly standard for both parties to keep confidential and never disclose the terms of settlement. Consequently, there are few published accounts of how these settlements actually occur. Among experienced defense attorneys, however, it is a well-settled truth that even the most vigorous plaintiff who may have demanded millions until the day the defendant won its summary judgment motion is often willing to settle for a "walk-away" settlement simply to avoid the prospect of facing a Rule 11 motion.

speculative to work. What the system needs is a mechanism that operates with a high degree of immediacy and certainty to raise the prospect of reimbursing the defendant's fees.

Modifications to the American Rule

The "pure" American rule is bad enough with the incentives it creates for the filing of weak claims and the delayed resolution of worthy claims, but Congress over the past 70 years or so has modified the American rule by statute, adopting a series of provisions that give plaintiffs the chance to recover their attorneys' fees without a corresponding chance for defendants. These one-way fee-shifting statutes specifically contemplate that a losing defendant pay the plaintiff's attorneys fees *in addition* to the plaintiff's compensatory damages and (where appropriate) punitive damages. These pro-plaintiff, one-way fee-shifting statutes obviously further increase the incentives for litigation. In many situations the presence of the one-way fee-shifting statute can create lawsuits where the plaintiff's attorneys are seeking to recover fees that are far in excess of the plaintiff's actual damages. In essence, one-way fee-shifting statutes create litigation for its own sake.

The genesis of these statutes is in the early 1900s as part of the "progressive" era of legislation. Congress and the state legislatures began creating regulatory agencies to monitor certain industries as well as the modern class action rules that were to facilitate mass litigation over consumer harms. At the same time, Congress and the legislatures also adopted rules in consumer and employee-protection statutes intended to help consumers and employees recover their damages from corporate defendants. The thinking at the time was that the balance of power too much favored defendants and prevented consumers and employees from enforcing their rights through the courts.

Today there are a number of statutes that specifically empower plaintiffs' attorneys to recover their fees in a case they win in addition to the plaintiff's recovery of compensatory and other damages, including:

- The Fair Labor Standards Act, the 1938 federal law that guarantees a minimum wage and requires employers to pay overtime wages to certain employees who work more than the maximum number of hours per week;[63]

- The Americans With Disabilities Act;[64]

- Title VII of the Civil Rights Act of 1964; and [65]

- The Age Discrimination in Employment Act.[66]

In a 1983 Supreme Court case interpreting the fee-shifting provisions of the Clean Air Act, the Supreme Court noted that there were more than 150 federal statutes (at that time) with one-way fee-shifting provisions.[67] California alone has several hundred one-way fee-shifting statutes.[68]

In addition, there are specific statutes in some states that allow plaintiffs to recover their attorneys' fees based upon the defendant's conduct in handling the plaintiff's claim but that do not allow a winning defendant to recover its attorneys' fees where the plaintiff has engaged in egregious conduct.[69] To reduce the incentives for parties to initiate litigation and to encourage the settlement of litigation at the earliest stages in the proceedings and to avoid situations where lawsuits become a vehicle dominated by the pursuit of attorneys' fees for their own sake, legislatures should (1) eliminate or restrict statutory provisions that allow plaintiffs to recover attorneys' fees in addition to their other damages and (2) adopt provisions that allow defendants to recover their attorneys' fees from plaintiffs when the defendant prevails.

Obviously these one-way fee-shifting rules simply exacerbate the problems created by the American rule, fueling the problem of excess litigation with incentives that guarantee the filing of additional lawsuits and delay the resolution of meritworthy claims.

---

63. Fair Labor Standards Act, 52 Stat. 1060 (June 25, 1938) codified at 29 U.S.C. 201 et seq. (hereinafter, the "FLSA"). Unlike some other fee-shifting statutes, however, while the court retains discretion over the amount of attorneys fees awarded, the award itself is mandatory under FLSA. *Fegley v. Higgins*, 19 F.3d 1126 (6th Cir. 1994) *cert. denied*, 513 U.S. 875 (1994).

64. Americans with Disabilities Act of 1990, 104 Stat. 327 (July 26, 1990) codified at 42 U.S.C. 12101 et seq.

65. Civil Rights Act of 1964, Pub. L. No. 88-352, codified in scattered sections of 42 U.S.C.

66. Age Discrimination in Employment Act of 1967, Pub. L. No. 90-202 codified at 29 U.S.C. 621 et seq.

67. *Ruckelshaus v. Sierra Club*, 463 U.S. 680 (1983).

68. Lorraine Wright Feuerstein, *Two-Way Fee Shifting on Summary Judgment or Dismissal: An Equitable Deterrent to Unmeritorious Lawsuits*, 23 PEPP. L. REV. 125, 150 n180 (1995).

69. In Georgia, for example, although a defendant cannot ordinarily recover its attorney's fees, the plaintiff may where it has requested it in the complaint and "where the defendant has acted in bad faith, has been stubbornly litigious, or has caused the plaintiff unnecessary trouble and expense". O.C.G.A. § 13-6-11.

5

Punitive Damages Are Out of Balance

[T]here is no evidence for a deterrent effect from punitive damages whatso-ever. There's no empirical study that's ever been done that shows that puni-tive damages have any constructive function. What we have now is a penalty system with no benefits and all costs. Professor Kip Viscusi, Harvard Law School, The Trouble With Lawsuits (1999).

Many of the advocates of litigation reform point to punitive damages as a key problem in the current system. Newcomers to litigation often think of punitive damages as something that plaintiffs have a right to collect as compensation for the harms done to them. Most of those newcomers would be surprised to learn that legal scholars think about punitive damages in a very different way.

The Purpose for Punitive Damages

The very heart of civil litigation is the plaintiff's claim that the defendant has injured it and that the plaintiff is entitled to compensation for that injury. In a breach of contract case, the measure of damages is usually the difference between the benefit the plaintiff would have received if the defendant had performed under the contract versus the benefit the plaintiff actually received. So, for exam-ple, if the contract required the defendant to deliver 10 widgets but the defendant delivered only five (assuming that the plaintiff actually paid for 10) the plaintiff's claim for damages is equal to the amount paid for the 5 missing widgets.

In a tort case, the plaintiff's damages are measured by the value of the thing that was lost or damaged as a consequence of the defendant's wrongdoing. Those damages may be both direct and indirect. Direct damages might include the plaintiff's medical expenses caused by the injuries that resulted from the defendant's wrongdoing. Indirect damages might include the loss of wages the plaintiff suffered during the time he was unable to work as a consequence of the defendant's wrongdoing.

In most states, a plaintiff can recover punitive damages only where the defendant's wrongdoing was "willful" or overcomes some other, higher-than-negligent, standard for bad conduct. That is, for an award of punitive damages, a defendant must be worse than negligent.

Because of this general rule, punitive damages are not available in a breach of contract case. Although creative plaintiff's attorneys often try to get around this general rule by claiming that the defendant's conduct was so egregious that it somehow constituted fraud (an intentional tort for which punitive damages may be awarded) for the balance of this chapter I will mostly be talking about punitive damages in tort claims cases.

There are several theories that proponents traditionally use to justify the concept of punitive damages. One is that by allowing the court to penalize a defendant who has engaged in reckless or intentionally wrongful conduct, the jury deters the same kind of reckless or wrongful conduct in the future. The possibility of punitive damages, in theory, should give manufacturers and producers of goods and services a strong incentive to avoid reckless or intentionally wrongful conduct. The occasional grant of punitive damages "sends a message" to the marketplace that defendants can face serious consequences if they misbehave.

A second argument is a variation on the first. It argues that litigation over actual damages is not enough, by itself, to deter wrongful conduct. Not every damaged plaintiff sues. Some plaintiffs never realize the source of their injuries and even some that do never exert the effort to bring the claim in litigation. As a result, if only some percentage of all the potential plaintiffs sued, and if those plaintiffs who did sue recovered only actual damages, there would be an "under-deterrence gap" equal to the actual damages suffered by all of the potential plaintiffs who never sued. The courts need awards of punitive damages, the argument goes, to overcome this under-deterrence gap or else manufacturers and producers will have an incentive to cut corners, putting profits ahead of safety.

The problem with both of these arguments is that there is mounting evidence that punitive damages do not motivate manufacturers and producers to increase safety and reduce risk.

The Effects of Punitive Damages

One of the leading scholars studying the punitive damages question is Professor Kip Viscusi from Harvard Law School. In a series of studies he examined the way juries make decisions involving punitive damages using a fixed set of hypothetical facts presented to a mock jury (much in the way marketing professionals use focus groups to test the viability of advertising campaigns).

In one of those tests, Viscusi's hypothetical proposed that there was an auto manufacturer with annual profits of $7 billion that had a particular line of cars that had a defective electrical system. The defective electrical system would occasionally start fires that sometimes resulted in horrible burns or even death for the passengers in the car. Altering the design of the car to avoid the defects in the electrical system would have cost $10 million for every 100,000 cars produced, or a cost of $100 per car. The company considered making the change, but then decided against it, reasoning that, even with the increased risk of death from the faulty electrical system, this particular line of cars had one of the best safety records in its class.[70]

The hypothetical tells the mock jurors that, after hearing the evidence in a case involving a passenger who died from a fire started by the faulty electrical system, the jury awarded the plaintiff $800,000 in damages. This amount represents the economic loss of the deceased and the pain and suffering for the deceased and his family. The test then asked the mock jurors whether they would award punitive damages in addition to this amount, and if so, how much.

Let's pause for a moment to ask what the jurors ought to do if the role of punitive damages is to deter wrongdoing. In this hypothetical case, the manufacturer could have avoided the injuries done to the plaintiff if it had spent $100 per car on a change in design. One way to consider deterrence would have been to determine what was the statistical likelihood of death or injury from the faulty electrical system so that the jury could determine, for every 100,000 cars sold, how many would result in an electrical fire that would cause injuries or death to the passengers. With that statistic in hand, the jury could compare the value of each life saved through the change in design versus the $10 million in cost per 100,000 cars that "saved life" would have cost. A punitive damages award that would serve to deter the manufacturer from choosing cost savings over safety would be one that was just enough to tip the economic scales.

---

70. W. Kip Viscusi, *The Trouble with Lawsuits* (1999), *available at* http://www. techcentralstation.com/052900C.html.

In Professor Viscusi's test he not only collected the opinions of the mock jurors in this hypothetical, but he also varied the test by telling some mock jurors that the manufacturer had performed a statistical analysis just like the one described above. In one of these variations, the mock jurors heard that the manufacturer determined that redesigning the electrical system would save the lives of 10 passengers but would cost a total of $40 million. The manufacturer valued each "saved life" at $3 million, a number used by the National Highway Traffic Safety Administration in valuing life in other safety contexts.

As you can see, in this variation of the hypothetical, the manufacturer did the right thing, from an economic point of view. If the value of each life saved was $3 million and the design changes would have saved 10 lives for a total of $30 million, but the design changes would have cost $40 million, the economically efficient outcome would have been to avoid the design change. In other words, it would have been economically more efficient to pay $30 million in damages for the 10 lost lives rather than pay $40 million to change the design and avoid their deaths.

In Professor Viscusi's study the jurors did almost the opposite of what they should have done if the purpose of punitive damages is deterrence. In the hypothetical where the manufacturer did not consider the economic value of the lives saved, the mock jurors awarded lower punitive damages. In each variation where the manufacturer undertook a benefit versus cost analysis, the mock jurors awarded more punitive damages. In those variations where the manufacturer undertook a benefit versus cost analysis and used a *higher* number for the economic value of each saved life, the mock jurors *increased* the punitive damages award on the company. As Professor Viscusi explained:

> "What's happening here is that the higher the figure used by the company in its analysis as the value of human life, the higher the baseline award that the jurors used to determine punitive damages. If a company used a $3 million value of life, the jurors reasoned that they had to "send the company a message", resulting in a damages award larger than $3 million. We are left with the perverse result that the more responsible the company is in one sense, in terms of using a higher value of life, the more it is penalized in terms of damages. So not only are you penalized for doing benefit cost analysis, but you're hit with higher damages awards if you value life by a greater amount."[71]

---

71. *Id.*

The psychological factor at play is what Professor Viscusi calls "hindsight bias". When mock jurors hear the story of a manufacturer who made a decision to avoid making a design improvement because of its cost, they are more inflamed when they hear that the manufacturer undertook a study of the cost and considered the value of saved lives than when the manufacturer undertook no such study. Moreover, the higher the value placed on human life by the manufacturer, the more inflamed the mock jurors became and the higher value they placed on the penalty (the punitive damages award).[72]

It's easy to see how an enterprising plaintiff's attorney would use exactly this kind of evidence to build a case for punitive damages in an actual trial. The plaintiff's attorney would waive the benefit cost studies in front of the jury, saying that the manufacturer had been "caught red-handed" and was guilty of putting a value on human life. To "send a message" that such cold-blooded conduct was unacceptable, the attorney would argue, the jury should award punitive damages because money is the only language the defendant will understand. You get the idea.

Unfortunately, however, this is exactly the wrong way to determine punitive damages and the fact that mock jurors actually use hindsight to craft punitive damages awards raises the question of whether punitive damages can play a role in the tort system. If all juries work the way the mock juries did in Professor Viscusi's study, then no manufacturer should ever undertake a benefit cost analysis. Manufacturers would place a value on human life only at their peril and should make certain never to consider how many lives might be saved if their products were changed or improved. And yet, that is exactly the opposite outcome that punitive damage awards are supposed to bring.

Interestingly, this phenomenon of the lack of linkage between punitive damages and deterrence is independent of the value choices inherent in any discussion of economic efficiency. I recognize that, in much of the discussion so far I have outlined how the macroeconomic cost of litigation acts as a drain on society as a whole, effectively drawing several hundred billion dollars of productive value out

---

72. The role of hindsight bias is not limited to juries. In one study of securities litigation another group of academics found that, although many judges recognized the potential for hindsight bias, they actually suffered from this form of bias themselves. And, where hindsight bias disconnects the potential for punitive damages from the choices market participants can make, it also eliminates the potential for punitive damages to deter wrongful conduct. *See* Mitu Gulati, Jeffrey J. Rachlinski, Donald C. Langevoort, *Fraud by Hindsight*, (Georgetown Law School, 2002) *available at* http://www.law.georgetown.edu/faculty/documents/gulati.pdf.

of the U.S. economy every year. Some opponents of reform might suggest that this is simply the wrong way to look at things. They might argue that, even if the overall system for litigating cases is inefficient in the sense of costing more than it produces, nevertheless it is somehow "just" or "fair". They would argue that punitive damages are appropriate because they punish bad behavior, even if they don't have the effect of actually deterring it. They would stress that there is a value inherent in punishing bad behavior—some concept of justice, perhaps—that is independent of the efficiency of the economic outcome.

Accepting the premises for the sake of argument, it is still not clear how the potential for punitive damages serves the value of justice (as articulated from the view of these opponents). In Professor Viscusi's study of mock jury awards, the size of the punitive awards increased if the manufacturer of the car performed a benefits cost analysis. The size of the punitive awards granted by mock juries increased further as the manufacturer increased its valuation for the cost of human life in its benefits cost analysis.[73] This means that, rather than punishing bad behavior, punitive damages awards often punish good behavior, namely the rigorous study and evaluation of potential risks, the evaluation of the harms that can flow from those risks and the study of possible preventions for those harms. In short, even if you wish to ignore the economic impacts of the role of punitive damages, it is not possible to construct a justification for punitive damages based on an ambiguous formulation of justice or fairness.

Although we've focused so far on tort claims involving safety, the same rationale applies in any other context in which punitive damages play a role. In any case in which the defendant is accused of intentional wrongful conduct, the plaintiff will be able to recover its actual damages and may also seek punitive damages. If punitive damages were a deterrent, they ought to equal the amount that, had the defendant considered it, would have been sufficient to persuade the defendant that the wrongful conduct was undesirable. If, however, jurors work from a perspective of hindsight bias, then punitive damages become random and indiscriminate. They lose the potential to deter when they cease to be clearly coupled to the action they intend to punish.

---

73.   W. Kip Viscusi, *Punitive Damages: How Jurors Fail to Promote Efficiency*, 39 HARV. J. OF LEGIS. 139 (2002).

Blockbuster Awards of Punitive Damages

How prevalent are massive awards of punitive damages and what relationship they play in contrast to the $286 billion in excess litigation costs each year?

As of April 2004, there have been sixty-four cases involving an award of punitive damages in excess of $100 million.[74] Of these sixty-four "blockbuster" awards, 95% were issued by juries (as opposed to judges acting in a trial without a jury). The first such award was issued in 1985 and the pace of awards over $100 million has accelerated since then. More than half of the 64 blockbuster awards occurred between 1999 and 2003. Measured in terms of dollars awarded, 90% of all of the blockbuster punitive damages awards were awarded between 1999 and 2003.[75] The 64 blockbuster awards totaled approximately $70 billion.

Understanding the economic impact of these massive awards can be difficult for several reasons. First, after an award of massive punitive damages there is often either an appeal by the defendant or a confidential settlement. (Because a winning plaintiff is aware of the possibility of losing the appeal and because of the time value of recovering an award sooner rather than later, even a winning plaintiff often has an incentive to settle at a significant discount from the actual award). Of the 64 blockbuster awards twenty-two cases were settled and fifteen of those settlements were confidential. Of the 42 remaining blockbuster awards a great many were appealed. In some, the award was reduced and then settled. In others the award was either reduced or affirmed. In five of the 42 cases the matter was the subject of an appeal that had not yet been decided. As a consequence, while a significant portion of the $70 billion in blockbuster awards remained outstanding after the exhaustion of appeals, efforts at reduction and settlements, it was unclear what would be the final amount.

A related analysis, however, suggests that the $70 billion level may tend to understate the impact of massive punitive damages awards. Often large corporate defendants in cases with the potential to result in punitive damages will settle those cases for amounts that exceed the plaintiff's actual economic damages simply to avoid the possibility of a far more excessive award of punitive damages "thus inducing a potential understatement of the total economic cost associated with large punitive damages awards."[76] As a result, while huge awards of punitive

---

74. W. Kip Viscusi, *The Blockbuster Punitive Damages Awards*, 53 EMORY L.J. 1405, 1409 (2004).

75. *Id.* at 1413.

76. *Id.* at 1415.

damages undoubtedly have a significant effect in many cases it is hard to put a definitive number on their economic effect.

Conceding that the aggregate effect is hard to quantify, however, does not mean that blockbuster punitive damages award are insignificant or play no role in the thinking of plaintiffs who decide to prosecute claims or defendants who agree to settle out of a fear of punitive damages. Even a handful of outrageous verdicts, delivered with enough regularity to develop a patina of propriety, can be enough to shift the perceptions of litigants.

What should be an appropriate level of punitive damages in a case brought against a car manufacturer alleging that the car's gas tank was designed poorly, contributing to the death of its driver and the burn injuries of other occupants when the car is rear-ended? Think of a number and then read the next few paragraphs.

Patricia Anderson was the driver of the 1979 Chevy Malibu that was rear-ended by a drunk driver in California. The parties' experts disputed whether the driver was going fifty or seventy miles an hour, but as a result of the impact the car's gas tank ruptured and burst into flames, killing the driver and injuring the surviving passengers.

Mrs. Anderson's estate sued General Motors, the manufacturer of the car, with her lawyers arguing that the design of the car placed the gas tank in the rear of the vehicle, making it more likely to rupture in the event of a rear-end collision and making GM responsible for the injuries of Mrs. Anderson and her passengers.

Remember the number I asked you to imagine a few paragraphs ago? The jury in *Anderson v. General Motors* imagined $4.9 billion in punitive damages. While that amount was later reduced by the court to $1.2 billion even that number is hard to fathom.[77] After all, people die in car accidents all the time. General Motors sells hundreds of thousands of cars every year. Should GM be obligated to dole out a billion dollars to every one who is injured or killed in one of its cars?

If you were the lead lawyer at GM handling claims like Mrs. Anderson's, how would you evaluate your potential liability after the loss you suffered in her case? How much more would you be willing to pay to settle the next case that came down the line? How much more would you be willing to settle a questionable case just to avoid the risk of going to trial?

---

77. Walter Olson, THE RULE OF LAWYERS 237-239 (2004).

Punitive Damages and Arguments from Equity

Opponents of reform might suggest that, even if juries sometimes follow the wrong thought process in determining to issue punitive damages awards, nevertheless the mere threat of punitive damages acts as a deterrent by giving manufacturers incentives to make their products as safe as possible. If so, you would expect to see a difference between safety rates in states that permit plaintiffs to recover punitive damages versus those in states that prohibit punitive damages. Again, the evidence doesn't support this conclusion.

Professor Viscusi examined both accidental death rates and insurance premiums in different states. (Insurance premiums operate as a proxy for safety, measuring the actuarial likelihood of economic loss due to the lack of safety.) His study concluded there was no statistical correlation between the accident and insurance rates in those states where punitive damages were prohibited versus those where plaintiffs were able to recover punitive damages.[78] He concluded:

> "I looked at insurance premiums, total insurance premiums, medical malpractice premiums, product liability premiums and other liability premiums. This was an analysis by state and I found that there's no difference in the performance of the states without punitive damages.... Well when I published this, we had a couple of hostile commentators on this paper...one of whom suggested that we can't find a deterrent effect because government regulation produces most of the safety benefits you might otherwise expect to find. I agree totally. It's not that punitive damages do nothing, but the effect is such a small fraction of the overall regulatory environment that it is undetectable. We have government regulation, we have market incentives, and we have private insurance incentives. Frankly, we don't need random large hits to companies to provide constructive incentives for corporate responsibility. The net result of the system now is that we have damages inflicted on corporations but because they're not systematically predictable and correlative with the actual behavior of companies there is no evident deterrent effect."[79]

Among all of the arguments against punitive damages, I find this the most persuasive: they don't make society any safer. This conclusion not only follows from Professor Viscusi's studies but also makes sense from practical experience. The in-house attorney of any company with hundreds of thousands of customers knows that the company has incentives to provide quality service to its customers. If one

---

78. W. Kip Viscusi, *Why There is No Defense of Punitive Damages*, 87 GEO. L.J. 381, 392 (1998).
79. *Id.*

of its products fails, it is more likely to fail many times than it is to fail just once. As a result, even a slight risk of failure can be extremely significant.

Most companies in the U.S. employ a variety of methods to ensure that their products perform as intended. Companies hire engineers to build the products, the product development process is documented and controlled to produce a quality result and personnel in the company have the unique responsibility for testing the product to make certain that it performs as intended. In many cases, when the product is ready for market, manufacturers use "beta testing:" a process whereby the product is used in real world conditions by a limited number of users to validate laboratory tests. Most companies employ these and other quality control methods because they don't want to sell a product that doesn't work. If the product fails, the company loses customer goodwill and the potential for future sales.

In addition to the up-side incentives provided by the goodwill of customers, companies are motivated to avoid the expense that accompanies customer-initiated litigation and claims for damages. When it comes to motivating quality control (which is synonymous for safety) the expense of litigation is motivation enough. The availability of punitive damages adds very little to that motivation. A customer claim for $1 million in economic damages will cost almost as much to litigate as if that claim were coupled with a demand for punitive damages. The punitive damages aspect of the case simply piles on the potential for more disruption in business if the company loses. If there is no demand for punitive damages, the case doesn't become less expensive to litigate. The same legal and factual issues are present in the case and the lawyers cost just as much to hire regardless of the amount at stake in the case. In short, the potential for punitive damages does not motivate firms to make their products better or safer although that potential does increase the prevalence of litigation, the size of attorneys' fees claims on the plaintiffs' side and the overall cost to society.

Recent Developments Involving Punitive Damages

In 2003 the United States Supreme Court had the opportunity to consider whether there were any Constitutional limitations on the ability of courts to impose punitive damages on defendants.[80] The Court's reasoning in that

---

80. *State Farm Mutual Automobile Ins. Co. v. Campbell*, 538 U.S. 408 (2003) (hereinafter, *State Farm*).

case—which applies in both state and federal cases—offers some insights into possible reforms.

The Supreme Court's decision arose out of an appeal by State Farm Automobile Insurance Co. from a ruling by the Utah Supreme Court. In the case, State Farm was accused of having exercised bad faith in its handling of an auto insurance policy held by its insured, Campbell. According to the facts summarized by the Utah Supreme Court, in 1981 Campbell tried to pass six vans on a two-lane highway. While trying to pass in the oncoming lane, another driver was forced to swerve onto the shoulder of the highway, hitting another car and dying in the collision. Mr. Campbell was uninjured, but was sued by the estate of the driver who died and by others who were injured in the collision. At issue in the claims against Mr. Campbell was his negligence in driving on the wrong side of the road and the role his driving played in causing the collisions that killed one driver and injured others.

In handling the claims of the deceased driver and the other injured persons, State Farm allegedly told their insured, Mr. Campbell, that his "assets were safe and that [he] had no liability for the accident, that [State Farm] would represent [his] interests and that [he] did not need to procure separate counsel". Thereafter, in the lawsuit by the injured drivers against Mr. Campbell, the injured drivers received an award of more than $180,000 (which amount was more than $130,000 above the limits of Mr. Campbell's $50,000) policy. Mr. Campbell subsequently sued State Farm for its handling of the matter under the theory that State Farm had shown bad faith in handling the matter (a theory of intentional tort that may lead to an award for punitive damages).

In the state court action by Mr. Campbell against State Farm in Utah, Mr. Campbell ultimately received an award of $1 million in compensatory (or economic) damages and a punitive damages award of $145 million. After the Utah Supreme Court approved those awards, State Farm sought to have the awards reviewed by the U.S. Supreme Court.

The U.S. Supreme Court reversed the ruling of the Utah Supreme Court, holding in a vote of 6-3 that the punitive damages award was so excessive that it offended the due process clause of the U.S. Constitution. What makes the *State Farm* decision important for the question of litigation reform is the reasoning behind the Court's decision.

In writing the decision for the six justice majority in *State Farm*, Justice Kennedy ruled that the Court's decision should be guided by a three-part test it adopted in an earlier ruling on the constitutionality of punitive damages.[81] That three-part test indicated that the defendant's rights to due process under the

Constitution would be infringed unless that court, in considering the permissibility of a punitive damages award, considered (1) the degree of reprehensibility of the defendant's wrongdoing, (2) the disparity between the actual or potential harm suffered by the plaintiff and the punitive damages award and (3) the difference between the punitive damages awarded by the jury and the damages authorized or permitted in other comparable cases.[82]

In applying this three-part test, Justice Kennedy began by observing that compensatory (or economic) damages "are intended to redress the concrete loss that the plaintiff has suffered" while "punitive damages serve a broader function; they are aimed at deterrence and retribution."[83] He wrote that the examination of the "reprehensibility" of the defendant's conduct was the most important part of the test and that reprehensibility was present where "the harm caused was physical as opposed to economic; the tortious conduct evidenced an indifference to or reckless disregard of the health or safety of others; the target of the conduct had financial vulnerability; the conduct involved repeated actions or was an isolated incident; and the harm was the result of intentional malice, trickery or deceit, or mere accident."[84] On this first prong of the test, Justice Kennedy noted that State Farm had acted wrongly but concluded that a smaller award would have served the state's legitimate interests in punishing this wrongful conduct.

Instead, Justice Kennedy wrote the case "was used as a platform to expose, and punish, the perceived deficiencies of State Farm's operations throughout the country. The Utah Supreme Court's opinion makes explicit that State Farm was being condemned for its nationwide policies rather than for the conduct directed towards the Campbells."[85] Justice Kennedy's reasoning contradicts the rationales for punitive damages offered by some opponents of reform: that punitive damages make up the difference between the actual damages suffered by the individual plaintiff at issue versus the defendant's savings in all of the other cases where it was not sued and required to pay actual damages (i.e., the so-called "under-deterrence gap").

For the Court, however, the Utah Supreme Court was not wrong because it misunderstood the economics of punitive damages, but because its theory of penalizing the "nationwide" practices of State Farm were outside the scope of the case. Justice Kennedy noted that many of the nationwide practices discussed in

---

81.   *BMW of North America, Inc. v. Gore*, 517 U.S. 559 (1996) (hereinafter, *Gore*).
82.   *Gore*, 517 U.S. 559 at 575.
83.   *State Farm*, 538 U.S. at 416.
84.   *Id.* at 419.
85.   *Id.* at 420.

the earlier proceedings included practices that were legal in other states. By holding up those other-state practices for condemnation in Utah, the Utah courts were effectively punishing State Farm for its practices in other states and in other cases that were not properly implicated in the Campbell case.

Taking up the second prong of the test, Justice Kennedy noted that the Supreme Court had, in the past, been reluctant to impose a mathematical formula to describe the ratio between actual damages and punitive damages. This, of course, is consistent with the overall philosophy of the Rehnquist court, which is generally conservative and tends to look towards the intent of the authors of the Constitution in interpreting its provisions. There is no language in the Constitution that prescribes how punitive damages should be awarded or that even contemplates limitations on punitive damages. Further, it would have been quite a stretch for the Court to find a mathematical limitation on punitive damages in light of the Court's other rulings in matters of Constitutional interpretation.[86] While the Court did not want to establish a precise mathematical formula, however, it did reason that "Our jurisprudence and the principles it has now established demonstrate, however, that, in practice, few awards exceeding a single-digit ratio between punitive and compensatory damages, to a significant degree, will satisfy due process."[87] In other words, while it is possible for the ratio of punitive to actual damages to exceed 10:1, that ratio represents the upper boundary of what Constitutional requirements of due process will permit.

Importantly, Justice Kennedy did not suggest that punitive damages awards in the range of 10:1 should be expected to be ordinary or normal. On the contrary, his conclusion was that there would be very few awards that could permissibly exceed a ratio of 9:1. Justice Kennedy cited an earlier case in which the Court "concluded that an award of more than four times the amount of compensatory damages might be close to the line of constitutional impropriety."[88] He discussed the history of prior cases in which the Court had approved awards where punitive damages were double or triple the amount of compensatory damages. While

---

86. Two of the three dissenting justices, Justices Scalia and Thomas, both indicated in their dissenting opinions that the Court's prior ruling in *Gore* was wrongly decided. Justice Thomas wrote, "I continue to believe that the Constitution does not constrain the size of punitive damages awards." 538 U.S. 429 (Thomas, J., dissenting). Justice Ginsberg, the third dissenter, also indicated that she did not believe the federal Constitution limited punitive damages awards and that any legal limits on such awards must be imposed by the states. 538 U.S. 430 (Ginsberg, J. dissenting).

87. 538 U.S. at 425.

88. *Id.* at 425, *citing Pacific Mut. Life Ins. Co. v. Haslip*, 499 U.S. 1 at 23-24 (1991).

there could be "no rigid benchmarks" for a ratio between compensatory and punitive damages, "ratios greater than those we have previously upheld may comport with due process where a particularly egregious act has resulted in only a small amount of economic damages."[89]

Ultimately, he reasoned, "When compensatory damages are substantial, then a lesser ratio, perhaps only equal to compensatory damages, can reach the outermost limit of the due process guarantee. The precise award in any case, of course, must be based upon the facts and circumstances of the defendant's conduct and the harm to the plaintiff."[90]

The three important principles to take away from this reasoning are that (a) the maximum appropriate ratio of punitive damages to compensatory damages should decrease when compensatory damages are "substantial", (b) when compensatory damages are "substantial", the maximum ratio of punitive damages to compensatory damages should be in the range of 1:1 and (c) punitive damages must always be based upon the facts and circumstances of the defendant's conduct and the harm to the plaintiff.

This reasoning repudiates much of the logic of the opponents of reform and supports the reasoning of those who would place limits on awards of punitive damages.

First, if the permissible ratio of punitive damages to compensatory damages must decrease as compensatory damages become more substantial, then the argument that punitive damages are appropriate as "society's retribution" for the harm done is rebuffed. If a plaintiff recovers a substantial award of compensatory damages then justice is, in large measure, done. An award of punitive damages to punish particularly reprehensible conduct may be as much as 100% of the compensatory damages but not more than that amount. From the Supreme Court's point of view, there is no need for a significant multiplier if a plaintiff receives an award of substantial compensatory damages.

Second, when considering the appropriateness of punitive damages from a Constitutional point of view, concerns arising from the defendant's financial resources, the defendant's profits or cost savings realized as part of its wrongful conduct are inappropriate. There are abundant examples of plaintiffs' attorneys who have made closing statements to juries suggesting that the corporate defendant made so much in annual profits and that the only way to punish its conduct should be to retrieve some percentage of those profits. Under the Supreme

89. *Id.*
90. *Id.* at 425.

Court's reasoning in *State Farm*, that kind of argument is not permitted by the Constitution. To the contrary, Constitutionally appropriate levels of punitive damages should be measured with a view towards the harm done to the plaintiff, rather than the profits or financial condition of the defendant.

Knowing that there is now an upper limit on Constitutionally permissible punitive damages awards suggests a number of alternative legislative reforms, as we'll discuss later in this book. But, if either the 10:1 or 1:1 limitations from *State Farm* had been in place for the past twenty years, would it have had an effect on any of the largest "blockbuster" punitive damages awards?

In the 2004 study mentioned above that compiled the list of the 64 punitive damages awards over $100 million, Professor Viscusi concluded that "The effect of *State Farm* on these blockbuster punitive damages awards was immediate."[91] He noted that two of the 64 cases had been awarded immediately prior to the release of the *State Farm* decision. In the first of these two cases, the jury had made a punitive damages award of $931 million, which represented a ratio of punitive damages to compensatory damages of 321:1. Shortly after the verdict the parties settled the case for $23 million. After giving effect to the jury's compensatory damages award of $2.9 million, this settlement amount implies a ratio of approximately 7:1.[92]

The second case was *Romo v. Ford Motor Co.*,[93] in which the jury verdict and appeal took place shortly after the *State Farm* decision was announced. What is especially interesting is the way in which the California Court of Appeals applied the Supreme Court's reasoning to reduce an award of $290 million to $23.7 million (which represented a ratio of 5:1):

> "First, we conclude…that the jury was fundamentally misinstructed concerning the amount of punitive damages it could award in the present case…. Accordingly, plaintiffs' counsel argued that the award should be large enough to force Ford to recall all remaining 1978-79 Broncos still on the road and "crush them to dust." Counsel argued that $1 billion was the appropriate award, based on the profit Ford made on all 1978-79 Broncos, factored to reflect Ford's use of that money over the next twenty years. Finally, counsel requested $1 billion so that the resulting publicity would reach all remaining owners of this model Bronco so that they would know how dangerous the vehicle was. These considerations are impermissible under *State Farm* and plaintiffs' arguments served to magnify the impact of the misinstruction."[94]

---

91. Viscusi, *Blockbuster Awards*, *supra* n74 at 1421.
92. *Id.*
93. *Romo v. Ford Motor Co.*, 113 Cal. App. 4th 738 (2003).

Looking retrospectively at the other 62 blockbuster punitive damages awards (which, collectively, amounted to approximately $70 billion) Professor Viscusi examined how these awards would have fared under a limit of 9:1 or 1:1. He concluded that if these cases were limited by a ratio of 9:1, more than half of the awards would have exceeded the limit and the $70 billion aggregate amount of the awards would have been reduced to approximately $14 billion. If the cases were limited by a ratio of 1:1, more than 90% of the cases and 90% of the $70 billion in damages would have exceeded the limit.[95]

One might fairly ask whether the blockbuster awards, because they are so large in dollar value are unusual in the way they exceed the single digit ratios now mandated by the Supreme Court's reasoning in *State Farm*. Professor Viscusi's study examined a large sample of punitive damages awards taken from state courts cases collected in 1996.[96] These punitive damages awards fell far below the $100 million "blockbuster" limit, with a median award of $50,000 in jury trials and $33,000 in trials before a judge. Of these state court awards, 96% were within the 9:1 ratio and 71% were within the 1:1 ratio, suggesting that punitive damages in state court cases with relatively modest overall awards were more balanced than the blockbuster awards. Even so, the aggregate value of the awards in the imbalanced cases was significant. The 29% of cases that exceeded the 1:1 ratio accounted for 94% of the total dollar value of all of the awards. Consequently, if 29% of the state court cases had been invalidated under the reasoning in *State Farm*, the aggregate amount of punitive damages awarded would have been reduced by a whopping 94%.

Professor Viscusi's study is not alone. Several years before the *State Farm* decision, two researchers undertook a similar study of California verdicts involving punitive damages.[97] Their study examined 489 cases between 1991 and 2000 in which California courts had awarded punitive damages. In those 489 cases, the total compensatory damages were approximately $840 million, but the aggregate punitive damages were $6.3 billion.[98] Examining all of the cases and the ratio between compensatory and punitive damages in each one revealed that slightly

94. *Id.* at 753-62.

95. Viscusi, *Blockbuster Awards, supra* n74 at 1422-1423.

96. *Id.* at 1423. See also Joni Hersch & W. Kip Viscusi, *Punitive Damages: How Judges and Juries Perform*, 33 J. LEGAL STUD. 1, 6 tbl. 1 (2004).

97. J. Clark Kelso and Kari C. Kelso, *An Analysis of Punitive Damages in California Courts, 1991–2000* (2001) *available from* http://www.cjac.org.

98. This number includes the $4.2 billion punitive award in *Anderson v. General Motors Corp.* discussed earlier, *supra* n77.

less than half of all these cases awarded punitive damages in excess of the 1:1 ratio.

These studies suggest that the imposition of a 1:1 cap on punitive damages will affect fewer than half of all cases that result in a punitive damages award but would significantly reduce the overall impact of punitive damages. In addition, under the opportunity curve model, having the plaintiff aware that punitive damages can never exceed compensatory damages would tend to depress the plaintiff's opportunity curve, encouraging resolution of cases earlier in the process.

The impact of the decision in *State Farm* doubtless will have a positive impact towards the goal of reducing punitive damages awards. What is less clear, however, is how consistently the reasoning in *State Farm* will be followed in the courts. While the discussion by the California Court of Appeals in *Romo* is heartening, there can be no guarantee that other state courts will be as faithful to Justice Kennedy's guidelines. The Supreme Court's role in the judicial system, generally, is to determine the broad outlines of what is permitted by the Constitution. Its role is not to set forth specific procedures or rules. This leaves, as we will see, a substantial area in which Congress and the States are free to adopt legislative guidelines to govern the courts in handling claims for punitive damages beneath the umbrella of what the Supreme Court has ruled the Constitution will permit.

6

Capping Punitive Damages

But Americans don't just sue big corporations or bad people. They sue doctors over misfortunes that no doctor could prevent. They sue their school officials for disciplining their children for cheating. They sue their local governments when they slip and fall on the sidewalk, get hit by drunken drivers, get struck by lightning on city golf courses...Many of these cases do not belong in court. But clients and lawyers sue anyway, because they hope they will get lucky and win a jackpot from a system that allows sympathetic juries to award plaintiffs not just real damages...but millions more for impossible-to-measure "pain and suffering" and highly arbitrary "punitive damages." Stuart Taylor Jr. and Evan Thomas, Civil Wars, NEWSWEEK (December 15, 2003).

The greatest impact of America's litigation burden comes from transaction costs (approximately $192 billion in 2002—consisting of defendants' and plaintiffs' attorneys fees) and noneconomic damages (approximately $61 billion in 2002—including both nonpecuniary damages and punitive damages). These costs are the primary contributors to the overall litigation inefficiency of $236 billion annually and probably do the most to contribute to any deadweight loss (which we've estimated at another $50 billion per year).[99]

Punitive damages not only make up a substantial portion of the total inefficiency of American litigation, but their availability increases the number of lawsuits filed and makes it more expensive to settle those claims. A plaintiff with a $10,000 claim who thinks it can get an additional $1 million in punitive damages may be unlikely to settle even if the defendant is willing to pay the entire amount of the plaintiff's actual damages. While it is difficult to quantify the impact that punitive damages have on the incidence or settlement value of litigation, Yale law professor George Priest has been quoted to say, "[T]he availability of unlimited punitive damages

---

99. *See* Figure 1.4.

affects the 95% to 98% of cases that settle out of court prior to trial. It is obvious and indisputable that a punitive damages claim increases the magnitude of the ultimate settlement and, indeed, affects the entire settlement process, increasing the likelihood of litigation."[100]

While some have suggested a variety of reforms—and we'll examine some of them in Chapter 8—the "low-hanging fruit" in this calculation is the transaction costs and punitive damages. The most effective reforms America could adopt, and those that would have the most significant and immediate effect, are those that would lower transaction costs and lower the rate of punitive damages. With respect to punitive damages, many states are already at work on reforms that should make a positive contribution.

Limitations on Punitive Damages

State legislatures have the power to set limits, by statute, on the way in which courts in their states can permit punitive damages, the amounts of those punitive damages, the standard of proof required to permit punitive damages and the way in which those punitive damages can be paid. *Appendix A* sets forth a list of all of the limitations on punitive damages that have been adopted in the 50 states and the District of Columbia.[101] The first column (entitled "any limit") merely notes whether the state has adopted any kind of restriction on punitive damages. The second column (entitled "ratio limit") notes whether the state has adopted a dollar limit on the amount of punitive damages that can be awarded. Such a limit might be expressed as "flat" (meaning that the statute prohibits punitive damages in excess of some flat dollar amount), or as a multiple of compensatory damages (expressed as 1x (one times), 2x (two times), etc.) and can be expressed as "variable" (where the limitation is more complicated; for example, a rule that limited punitive damages to 3 times compensatory damages up to a maximum of $1 million would be noted as "3x, variable").

The third column (entitled "std of proof") notes where the legislature requires a higher standard of proof in cases involving punitive damages. In civil cases, to prevail on its claims a plaintiff ordinarily must prove its case by a "simple preponder-

---

100. http://www.atra.org/show/7343.
101. The table in *Appendix A* is derived from a similar table maintained by the American Tort Reform Association but I have expanded it to differentiate between different types of limitations on punitive damages and also to provide notes and citations where available.

ance" of the evidence, meaning that the plaintiff has more evidence of its story than does the defendant. In states where the "std of proof" column is marked with an "X", the legislature has provided that the court may approve an award of punitive damages only where the plaintiff can prove that the defendant acted with a heightened level of wrongdoing (usually "intentional" wrongdoing or "reckless" wrongdoing) to a degree of certainty that is higher than a simple preponderance of the evidence (usually by a showing of "clear and convincing" evidence).

Examining how states have adopted limitations on punitive damages to date suggests some additional limitations that might be effective at limiting the overall level of punitive damages and appropriate in light of the Supreme Court's recent guidance in its *State Farm* decision.

Heightened Standards of Proof

The limitation on punitive damages that is probably the least likely to limit the number of lawsuits filed or encourage their early settlement or resolution is a requirement that punitive damages be proven with a heightened standard of proof. Nineteen states have adopted such a heightened standard of proof and nearly all of these require proof by a showing of "clear and convincing" evidence.

The problem with a limitation based on a standard of proof is that it is inherently amorphous and subject to interpretation. A plaintiff who is inclined to begin a lawsuit and who truly believes in the rightness of his position will be inclined to believe that he can satisfy the heightened standard. To the extent that the plaintiff might actually be wrong, the evidence required to overcome the plaintiff's initial belief about punitive damages will generally not become apparent until after the discovery phase of the case, by which time the parties will have hardened their positions and become emotionally wedded to those positions. Even more importantly, whether the court believes that a particular plaintiff has proven its case for punitive damages will be difficult to discern until the very end of the trial process and perhaps not until the court actually rules on the matter after the trial. The difference between proof by a simple preponderance and proof by clear and convincing evidence is largely a matter of perception and subjective bias. Consequently, limitations based upon a heightened requirement of proof, while they may hold some appeal from a sense of fairness or justice, are relatively unlikely to have a significant impact on the overall incidence of litigation.

Diversion Requirements

One type of limitation adopted by a number of states is a requirement that some percentage of any award of punitive damages be paid to a state fund. The thinking behind this kind of limitation is two-fold. First, to the extent that the state entitles itself to take a "cut" on any plaintiff's recovery of punitive damages, that approach is consistent with the theory of punitive damages as a form of deterrent. The plaintiff, after all, is fully compensated for its actual damages (medical expenses, injuries, lost wages, etc.) by an award of compensatory damages. From the plaintiff's point of view, an award of punitive damages is pure windfall. From the defendant's point of view, an award of punitive damages is punishment, imposed for the purpose of satisfying society's demand for retribution and in the hopes that such awards deter future defendants from the kind of wrongdoing alleged against the defendant in the case. By the state's taking a percentage of the punitive damages award, the state is, essentially, acting on the part of society itself in claiming the proceeds.

In addition, to the extent that reformers intend limitations on punitive damages to discourage litigation in general, diverting the proceeds of punitive damages awards may do just that. A plaintiff who perceives an opportunity to recover punitive damages perceives that opportunity as tending to raise the plaintiff's opportunity curve, thereby tending to increase the plaintiff's settlement demands and increasing the plaintiff's preference for litigation. By diverting a percentage of any recovery of punitive damages to the state, the state tends to depress the plaintiff's opportunity curve, driving down the plaintiff's settlement demands and driving down the plaintiff's preference for litigation.

As of July 2004, six states had in effect a requirement that some portion of a punitive damages award be diverted to a state fund. Indiana and Iowa, on one end of the spectrum require that 75% of the award go to the state while New York takes only 20%. Oregon has the most unusual diversion requirement, taking 60% of the punitive damages award for its state fund but prohibiting the prevailing attorney from taking more than 20% of the total punitive damages award.

These kinds of limitations, however, have been attacked as violating various state constitutions. In at least two situations—Georgia and Colorado—legislatures have adopted statutes requiring the payment of punitive damages awards to a state fund only to have courts in those states rule the statute to be unconstitutional.

It is unclear how effective diversionary schemes are at limiting the overall incidence of litigation. While the prospect of losing a percentage of a punitive damages award may tend to reduce the plaintiff's perceived opportunity curve, this back-end prospect may be too distant to have an immediate impact on a plaintiff's decision-making, particularly with respect to the decision to file a complaint or not. Diversionary plans ranging from 20% to 75% are, in one manner of thinking, like an income tax on the recovery and a plaintiff who hopes to recover a punitive damages award of up to 9 times compensatory damages may not perceive a loss of incentive if that award is reduced by half. The plaintiff would still be receiving a windfall of several times his compensatory damages, leaving a fairly significant incentive to litigate.

Even more importantly, a diversion requirement has no impact on the defendant's evaluation of a case. The prospect of a substantial punitive award may sometimes bring a defendant to settle a questionable or marginal case and, in a macroeconomic sense, those settlements are undesirable. Diverting a portion of a windfall award of punitive damages may remove some of the plaintiff's incentive but removes none of the leverage the plaintiff has over the defendant in provoking settlement. Consequently, diversion requirements still leave much to be desired when viewed as a means by which to lower the overall inefficiency of litigation.

Ratio Limits

Perhaps the most effective limitation on punitive damages, particularly in light of the Supreme Court's guidance in the *State Farm* case, is a limitation that is based upon the ratio between punitive damages and compensatory damages.

Thirty-four states have adopted some kind of statutory limit on punitive damages in the form of either a maximum amount of punitive damages or a maximum ratio of punitive damages to compensatory damages. In most of these states, the limit is variable, requiring, for example, that punitive damages not exceed the greater of (a) an amount equal to three times the compensatory damages or (b) a specified dollar amount.[102] Of the thirty-four states that have adopted some sort of cap, only three have had the cap declared unconstitutional by the state's appellate courts.

---

102. Arkansas's statute is a representative example of this kind of formula. In Arkansas, except in special circumstances, an award of punitive damages may not exceed the greater of (a) $250,000 or (b) the amount that is three times the amount of compensatory damages up to a maximum of $1 million. Special circumstances that can result in an uncapped punitive damages award exist when the court "determines by clear and convincing evidence that, at the time of the injury, the defendant intentionally pursued a course of conduct for the purpose of causing injury or damage". Arkansas Stat. 16-55-208.

Of the thirty-one states with caps that have survived constitutional challenges to date, the vast majority are variable caps based upon a maximum ratio of punitive to compensatory damages, subject to a maximum dollar limit. The ratio ranges from 5:1 at the high end to 1:1 at the low end, with an average around 3:1. Two states have flat dollar limits on maximum punitive damage awards (Georgia, $250,000 and Virginia, $350,000). One state, New Hampshire, prohibits awards of punitive damages altogether. Two states—Kansas and Mississippi—have limitations on punitive damages that are based on the defendant's finances, with the Kansas limitation based on the defendant's income and the Mississippi limitation based on the defendant's net worth. A handful of states have special limitations on punitive damages that apply only in specific types of cases.[103]

The viability of many of these state caps on punitive damages under the U.S. Constitution is unclear after the Supreme Court's decision in *State Farm*. Although the *State Farm* decision did not adopt a mathematical formula for the calculation of punitive damages awards based upon their relation to compensatory damages, the Supreme Court's reasoning suggested that most awards of punitive damages should be in the range of a 1:1 ratio with compensatory damages and that in rare cases the ratio could reach 9:1 or even higher. Nearly all of the state caps on punitive damages provide a simple mathematical formula, allowing the potential for punitive damages awards that might fall within the state's statutory limit but run afoul of the federal Constitutional limits announced in *State Farm*.

For example, in Idaho, the limit on punitive damages is the greater of (a) $250,000 or (b) an amount that is three times the compensatory damages.[104] Under this rule, an Idaho court might permit a punitive damages award of $250,000 in a case where the plaintiff's compensatory damages were only $10,000 and that award would be clearly permitted by the Idaho statute. The ratio of punitive to compensatory damages would be 25:1, which would almost certainly defy the federal constitutional limits prescribed by *State Farm*. This potential problem can arise in any state where the limitation on punitive damages is couched in terms of the "greater of" the specified ratio or a dollar amount.

In those states where the limit on punitive damages is based on some other fact (either a flat dollar amount as in Georgia and Virginia or an amount based upon the

---

103. In Alaska, for example, while the general limitation on punitive damages ranges from three times to four times the amount of compensatory damages, in a case for unlawful employment practices the cap on punitive damages ranges from $200,000 to $500,0000 based upon the number of employees the defendant has in the state. Alaska Stat. 9-17-020(h).

104. Idaho Stat. 6-1604(3).

defendant's finances as in Kansas and Mississippi) the state's limitation may also run afoul of the new Constitutional limits. In Georgia, for example, a punitive damages award of $250,000 in a case where compensatory damages were only $10,000 would satisfy the Georgia statute but generate a ratio of 25:1 that would almost certainly be unconstitutional under *State Farm*. Likewise, punitive damages that might be permitted under the Mississippi or Kansas rules because they are not linked to compensatory damages could easily exceed the single-digit ratios prescribed by *State Farm*.

Importantly, however, the constitutional limits prescribed in *State Farm* may not always result in an overall punitive damages award that is less than what state statutes would permit. The rule in *State Farm* does not address the dollar value of the punitive award and, in a case where compensatory damages are massive, the punitive award may also be massive. States that limit punitive damages under a "greater of" scheme may limit awards to amounts that are less than what *State Farm* would have permitted. Also, those states whose limits are unrelated to compensatory damages (whether based on a flat dollar amount or the defendant's financial condition) may well reduce punitive damages awards in cases where a rule based solely on ratios would have permitted a higher award. Although modifying caps on punitive damages to account for the reasoning of *State Farm* should reduce the overall burden of punitive damages (approximately $61 billion in 2002) it will not necessarily reduce punitive damages in every individual case.

A Proposed Model Cap on Punitive Damages

To achieve the twin goals of reducing the incidence of litigation by depressing the plaintiff's perceived opportunity for financial windfall and reducing the overall societal burden of punitive damages, states should consider adopting a new form of cap on punitive damages based upon the Supreme Court's reasoning in *State Farm*. I have provided a model statute that follows this approach in *Appendix B*.

The Model Statute accomplishes several goals. First, it establishes a baseline for punitive damages equal to one times compensatory damages, a level that is suggested by the reasoning in *State Farm*. Second, it contemplates situations in which punitive damages may exceed the 1:1 ratio and stipulates the situations where a higher award may be justified. The language in Section 1(b) of the Model Statute follows the language suggested in *State Farm*'s discussion of the elements of "reprehensibility".[105]

---

105. *State Farm, supra* n80 and discussion following.

Some legislatures may wish to augment the Model Statute with a further dollar limitation on punitive damages. Such a limit would further cap punitive damages in a "blockbuster" case where the compensatory damages themselves were massive. To do so, drafters could add a Section 2 to the Model Statute that imposes a flat dollar limit that would come into play only in situations where the ratio-driven limits on punitive damages would otherwise permit a dollar award that was too high. Such dollar value limitations on damages are more properly addressed by the states, based upon local attitudes and beliefs and other factors at play in the state. Some states with dollar value limits may want to adopt a periodic review of the dollar amount or may stipulate that the dollar value rise or fall with inflation or some other economic indicator.

What is important about this new approach of capping punitive damages is that it will eliminate the potential for ambiguity or uncertainty surrounding existing laws, nearly all of which were adopted before *State Farm*. By eliminating the potential for uncertainty, legislatures will not only ensure that their statutes will continue to be enforceable under the U.S. Constitution but by doing so they will cause potential plaintiffs to perceive more immediately the impact of this change in the law to their prospects for a windfall recovery. By creating an immediate impact on the perceived opportunity curves of potential plaintiffs, legislatures that adopt the Model Statute will encourage potential plaintiffs either to resolve their claims before litigation is begun or at a relatively early stage in the litigation. In addition, by reducing the overall value of punitive damages awards, states that adopt the Model Statute will help to reduce the overall societal impact of punitive damages awards by anywhere from $5 billion to $45 billion per year.[106]

---

106. In Chapter 5 we discussed Professor Viscusi's study of state court punitive damages awards in which he concluded that a 1:1 ratio of punitive to compensatory damages would have eliminated approximately 94% of those awards. If only ten percent of the $61 billion in annual noneconomic awards were punitive damages awards, 94% of the annual punitive damages awards would amount to $5 billion per year. If 90% of the $61 billion is punitive damages, around $45 billion per year would be excluded if all state courts limited punitive damages to one times compensatory damages. *See also*, Mark A. Klugheit, *Where the Rubber Meets the Road: Theoretical Justifications vs. Practical Outcomes in Punitive Damages Litigation*, 52 Syracuse L. Rev. 803 (2002) (concluding that a "legislative anchoring of punitive damage awards to a multiple of compensatory damages...or some other objectively ascertainable point of reference" would be the "simplest" way to weaken the *in terrorem* effect of punitive damages and to ensure that "punitive damages are awarded for legitimate purposes of social policy, rather than as sporadic windfalls for plaintiffs.").

7

Shifting Attorneys' Fees

The practical case for loser-pays is equally compelling. Litigants naturally think too well of their cases; loser-pays pushes them to size up their prospects more realistically. It also curbs the brand of extortion, so routine in American law as almost to have lost its ethical taint, by which lawyers use the costs of the process itself, or the risk of a fluke outcome found in any trial, to strong-arm their opponents into settlement. Walter Olson, Civil Suits, REASON (June 1995).

An even more effective proposal for reducing the overall incidence of litigation has two parts: (a) modifying existing one-way fee-shifting statutes that allow plaintiffs to recover their fees in a prevailing case but contain no reimbursement for winning defendants and (b) adopting new statutes that allow defendants to shift their fees to plaintiffs in cases where the defendants prevail. Perhaps even more than capping punitive damages, adopting rules that shift the burden of transactions costs onto the parties who initiate litigation would have the greatest and most immediate impact on reducing transactions costs and the overall burden of litigation.

Replace One-Way Fee-Shifting Statutes

As we discussed in Chapter 4, under the American rule, in nearly all civil litigation each party bears its own costs and attorneys' fees, regardless of the outcome. This allows a plaintiff to initiate litigation and extract a settlement from a defendant—even where the plaintiff has a tenuous or even frivolous case—because the defendant wants to avoid the cost of attorneys' fees and because the plaintiff is able to leverage the defendant's need for cost-avoidance. The incentive to litigate is even stronger for those plaintiffs whose claims are amenable to contingent fee arrangements because those plaintiffs can resort to litigation with virtually no cost at all, allowing them to perceive an opportunity curve from litigation that is nearly flat. That is, the potential for recovery without any fear of loss and without any cost: a situation that rewards the plaintiff for beginning litigation and continuing its case until the plaintiff believes it has maximized its value. These economic incentives are further exacerbated by a number of statutes that provide for "one-way fee-shifting", requiring defendants to pay the attorneys' fees of plaintiffs in certain kinds of cases.

The Fair Labor Standards Act (or "FLSA") is one of the best examples of a one-way fee-shifting statute that creates incentives for inefficient litigation. There have been numerous cases under the FLSA where attorneys initiated litigation on behalf of a supposed class of employees only to have the claims mostly disintegrate for lack of proof, leaving a small handful of employees with claims that, in the aggregate, were much less than the attorneys' fees being claimed in the case.

Because the FLSA was adopted in 1938, many of its provisions for the classification of workers as "exempt" (those salaried employees who do not need to be paid extra wages for overtime work) and "non-exempt" (those who must be paid 1.5 times their ordinary wage for each hour over 40 hours per week) are very difficult to apply. Jobs that are prevalent in our current economy (especially those involving computers and the Internet) did not exist in 1938 and the classifications Congress adopted in 1938 simply don't provide workable analogs in the twenty-first century. Although Congress amended some job classifications in 2004 to broaden the "white collar exemption" to the overtime rules, the FLSA remains an archaic piece of legislation that is very difficult for employers to implement in a digital economy.

In some of the more outrageous cases, plaintiffs' attorneys have initiated litigation only to learn—after several years of litigation—that what they thought was a class of many employees in fact includes only a small handful. The result may be a very small award to the employees but attorneys' fees may amount to ten or more times the employees' award.[107]

Because its fee awards are mandatory, the fee-shifting provisions of the FLSA are an especially wasteful example of litigation that primarily serves to generate attorneys' fees. In one case under the FLSA, the plaintiff employee won only $830.57 in compensatory damages but his attorney received a fee award of $13,032.[108]

---

107. Under the FLSA, an employee who is owed unpaid overtime can sue to recover two times the amount of overtime that should have been paid.

108. *Mazut v. Colonial Park Properties, Inc.*, No. 03-15009, 2004 WL 422029 (9th Cir. Sept. 9, 2004) (unpublished).

Because the statutes that allow some plaintiffs to recover their attorneys' fees in addition to their compensatory damages are scattered in hundreds of federal laws and various state laws as well, there can be no model statute that addresses all of them. Instead, Congress and the state legislatures should re-consider statutes that currently allow fee-shifting only to the plaintiff to see whether the conditions that originally prompted the statute are justified. In many instances, the conditions that may once have justified one-way fee-shifting may no longer prevail.

As part of that re-consideration, Congress and the state legislatures should consider statutory limitations on awards of attorneys' fees in those statutes that do allow plaintiffs to recover attorneys' fees. While supporters of these statutes can argue, with some justification, that certain kinds of pro-consumer and pro-employee cases require the awarding of attorneys' fees in order to make it possible for individual consumers and employees to pursue those cases, there can be no justification for statutes that allow attorneys' fees to exceed the recovery allowed for the consumer or employee. In those situations where an individual plaintiff's recovery is very small, attorneys can organize the case as a class action. If the plaintiffs' attorneys' fees dwarf the amount of the class recovery, then perhaps this is a matter more properly addressed by regulatory enforcement, rather than by private action.

In the cases discussing awards of attorneys' fees in pro-plaintiff fee-shifting statutes, judges have developed a series of tests for determining the propriety of fee awards. While those tests vary among the states, and under the federal statutes can vary based upon the statute, generally speaking these tests consider:

- The relationship between the fee award and the recovery received by the plaintiff;

- The amount of effort undertaken by the plaintiff's attorney to generate the plaintiff's recovery;

- The difficulty of the issues presented in the case and the quality of the work done by the plaintiff's attorney;

- The effective hourly rate that the fee award would imply (comparing the total award to the number of hours actually worked by the plaintiff's attorney); and

- The recovery that the plaintiff could have obtained earlier in the proceedings and the additional amount, if any, generated by the subsequent litigation.

While these judicial tests may sometimes be helpful in restraining the fee demands of plaintiffs' attorneys after the plaintiff has won a recovery, they do not serve as an effective means of limiting the demands of those attorneys in settlement discussions prior to trial. Those demands are unconstrained because the court retains so much discretion in determining the amount of the fee award. Consequently, a plaintiffs' attorney can hold out hope for a substantial fee award regardless of the amount of the plaintiff's recovery. Some judges may apply the multi-part test in a way that awards winning plaintiffs' attorneys the equivalent of hundreds of dollars per hour for every hour worked even though that aggregate amount may dwarf the amount of the plaintiff's recovery. Other judges may use the multi-part test to reduce the fee award to an amount that is 30% or 40% of the plaintiff's recovery, even though, when measured in dollars-per-billable hour, the attorneys' fees are quite low. The wide disparity in results in actual cases leaves both plaintiffs and defendants with uncertainty and an inability to predict the outcome. Because the disparity in outcomes is so great, the uncertainty is significant. Plaintiffs' attorneys often try to use that uncertainty as leverage in settlement discussions to extract a settlement that includes both a recovery for their client as well as a fee award that covers a full billable rate per hour.

This outcome is not only undesirable for the corporate employers who are most often the defendant in these cases, but also for the plaintiffs—both employees and consumers—as well. If a case reaches a stage where both parties effectively acknowledge the amount actually due to the plaintiff, the defendant has an incentive to acknowledge that liability and pay to settle the case. Settlement benefits the defendant by eliminating uncertainty and the ongoing cost of defense. If the plaintiff's attorneys, however, believe they can increase their own recovery of fees by continuing the litigation, they have an incentive to do so until they maximize their own recovery from the case. As a result, even though the corporate defendant may be willing to pay the plaintiff the amount the plaintiff believes is due, the plaintiff's attorney can stretch out the litigation to increase the possibility of an award of attorneys' fees at the expense of both the defendant and his own client.

To reduce this inefficiency, Congress and the state legislatures should consider a statutory limit on fee awards that adopts into law the multi-part tests that courts have already adopted in their own considerations. Doing this would not change the substantive law but it would formalize the decision-making process for judges when issuing fee awards. One possible formulation of a statutory guideline for fee awards would be to authorize judges to exercise their discretion in considering the multi-part test, subject to an overall limit that was equal to a percentage of the plaintiff's recovery. By formalizing the test for fee awards and limiting judicial discretion this reform would reduce the uncertainty that permeates pro-plaintiff fee-shifting statutes and would tend to encourage settlement at earlier stages in the litigation.

Fee-Shifting Under the English Rule

In addition to eliminating one-way fee-shifting rules (or making them two-way) legislators should consider adopting the English rule to further reduce the volume and cost of litigation.

Such a reform would dramatically alter the plaintiff's opportunity curve, tending to steepen the slope of the curve and increasing the plaintiff's urgency for settlement. At the same time, a pure loser-pays rule carries with it a certain logical elegance where the party who initiates the litigation takes on the risk that it may have to pay the defendant for the costs it is causing the defendant to incur.

Loser-Pays Efforts in Congress

Although the English rule was once thought to be a political third rail it is less so now and may even enjoy some political momentum. As Olson and Bernstein described in 1996, a federal loser-pays rule was part of the GOP's Contract With America in the 1994 congressional elections.[109] Under the title of the Attorney Accountability Act in 1995 House Republicans introduced a bill that would have adopted a loser-pays rule together with some other procedural reforms.[110] The measured passed in the House by a mostly party-line vote but only after being watered-down through a series of amendments. One of the strangest of those amendments was one that would have had the provision apply to suits filed directly in federal court, but not those that were originally filed in state court but subsequently removed to federal court under the principle of diversity jurisdiction.[111] This would have had the strange effect of giving the plaintiff the choice of whether to have the loser-pays rule govern his case, since the plaintiff would control the decision of whether originally to file in state court or federal court. Such an outcome, of course, would have been absurd.

---

109. Olson and Bernstein, *Loser-Pays, supra* n36.
110. H. R. 988, 104th Cong., 1st Sess. (1995).
111. Olson and Bernstein, *Loser-Pays, supra* n36 at 1174.

Ultimately the 1995 Attorney Accountability Act did not become law, but its passage through the House (even in its painfully amended form) and the lessons learned along the way suggest that the loser-pays rule may still be an option. Some were surprised that the GOP included the loser-pays rule in the 1994 Contract With America because, unlike issues like national defense and cutting taxes, it was not the kind of issue that had captured popular attention in the past. The Republicans who developed the platform, however, had been careful to test each of their positions with focus groups and must have thought that the issue had popular appeal.

Accordingly to Olson and Bernstein, the popular support for loser-pays depended on how the issue was phrased.[112] In a 1995 U.S. News and World Report survey, respondents were asked for their opinion in two different ways. In the first instance, respondents were asked, "If you sue someone and lose the case, should you pay his costs?" When asked this way, 44% agreed that they should pay the winner's costs. Alternatively, when respondents were asked, "If someone sues you and you win the case, should he pay your legal costs?" 85% of respondents answered yes.[113] When these results are averaged, they show clear support for a loser-pays rule.

Since the Attorney Accountability Act floundered in 1995, there has been little interest in a loser-pays rule in Congress even though the question of litigation reform has from time to time resurfaced.

Loser-Pays Rules in the States

At the state level, the only true loser-pays rule existing in a state code today is the Alaska rule. The Act of Congress that made Alaska a U.S. territory in 1900 specified that the winner of a lawsuit in Alaska courts would be entitled to collect his attorneys' fees from the loser.[114] Although the rule, currently found in Rule 82 of the Alaska Rules of Civil Procedure, has received a fair amount of attention and modifications over the past decade it still represents a good example of this kind of reform.[115]

As it now stands, except for special situations that are carved out of the general provisions of Rule 82, a plaintiff in an Alaska civil case who prevails and receives

---

112. *Id.* at 1172.
113. *Id.*, *citing* Stephen Budiansky et al., *How Lawyers Abuse the Law*, U.S. News & World Rep., Jan 30, 1995 at 50.
114. Olson and Bernstein, *Loser-Pays, supra* n36 at 1180.
115. *Id.* 1181-1186 (discussing the history of the 1993 amendments to Rule 82).

a judgment is entitled to an award of attorneys' fees on a sliding scale, depending on the stage of litigation at which the plaintiff won. The attorneys' fees are measured as a percentage of the judgment awarded (including prejudgment interest if included in the award), with the percentage decreasing in inverse proportion to the size of the judgment, and increasing based upon the stage of the litigation in which the case is resolved in three stages: non-contested, contested without trial and contested with trial as follows:[116]

Judgment and, if awarded, Prejudgment Interest	Contested With Trial	Contested Without Trial	Non-Contested
First $ 25,000	20%	18%	10%
Next $ 75,000	10%	8%	3%
Next $400,000	10%	6%	2%
Over $500,000	10%	2%	1%

These percentages, of course, apply only in situations where a party prevails and obtains a money judgment. In cases where the party defending the claim prevails, that party is entitled to 30% of its actual attorneys' fees if the case went to trial and 20% of its actual attorneys' fees if the case was resolved prior to trial.[117] Before Rule 82 was amended in 1993, a prevailing party who avoided a judgment against it was entitled to recover its reasonable attorneys' fees and Alaska courts had customarily granted between 40% and 80% of a winner's attorneys' fees in those cases.[118]

While Alaska's loser-pays rule has been somewhat diluted through the 1993 amendment which effectively limits the ability of a defending party from recovering more than 30% of its actual attorneys' fees, it still stands alone as an example of a loser-pays rule in the U.S. Alaska's offer of judgment rule (which we'll discuss below) in combination with the loser-pays effect of Rule 82 serve as some of the best examples of deterrents among the state rules in effect today.

While there is theoretical merit to the loser-pays rule, a pure English rule in American courts would require a huge change in the American litigation system. An effort to adopt the English rule would unite the plaintiffs' lawyers lobby with consumer interests and other groups. Because the change would have the facial

116. Alaska R. Civ. P. 82(b)(1).
117. Alaska R. Civ. P. 82(b)(2).
118. Kevin M. Kordziel, *Note, Rule 82 Revisited: Attorney Fee Shifting in Alaska*, 10 ALASKA L. REV. 429 at 437 (1993).

appearance of a significant departure from the status quo, opponents would label the measure "radical" and would oppose it vigorously. However much reformers might like the intrinsic simplicity of the loser-pays rule—and whatever the actual merits of such a change—it is difficult to imagine that Congress and the state legislatures could ever bring themselves to adopt so dramatic a change.

An alternative that should have substantially the same effect, but with a different political profile, would be an offer of judgment rule. At its heart, this reform would allow a defendant to make an offer of judgment to the plaintiff. If the plaintiff accepted the offer, the matter would be concluded and the defendant would be legally bound to pay the amount of the offer. If the plaintiff declined the offer, however, it would be free to pursue its claims through the litigation process but would be obligated to bear the attorneys' fees of the defendant from the point of the offer to the close of the case if the plaintiff's eventual recovery was less than the amount offered by the defendant.

For example, imagine a plaintiff with a tort claim against a defendant. The plaintiff began the litigation process, hiring a lawyer on a contingent fee basis, in the hopes of recovering $250,000 in medical expenses, lost wages and lost future earnings capacity. Although the plaintiff's complaint includes allegations of intentional tort, in order to raise the potential for punitive damages, privately the plaintiff and its attorney know that it will be hard to prove a case of intentional wrongdoing. The corporate defendant believes it has some possible dispositive legal arguments that give it a 25% chance of dismissing the case at summary judgment. The corporate defendant believes that, if it goes to trial, it will have only a 10% chance of winning a defense verdict because the plaintiff's injuries will make it appear fairly sympathetic to the jury. The corporate defendant believes it will cost $100,000 in attorneys' fees to manage the case to the summary judgment stage and an additional $100,000 thereafter if the case goes to trial.

The corporate defendant, however, knows that under the American rule even if it wins at trial and owes the plaintiff nothing, it will still be left with $200,000 in attorneys' fees. From the plaintiff's point of view, a settlement that got the plaintiff all or nearly all of its $250,000 in compensatory damages without the commitment of time, delay and uncertainty surrounding litigation would be a favorable outcome.

Shifting Fees Through an Offer of Judgment Rule

Under an offer of judgment rule, the defendant could make a written offer of judgment to the plaintiff (say, $50,000 or $100,000). The offer would remain open for a limited period of time as prescribed in the statute. The plaintiff would then have the choice of accepting the offer and concluding the case for that amount or continuing the litigation with the possibility of having to reimburse the defendant's attorneys' fees from the point of the offer onward. To assist in understanding the offer of judgment rule and as a suggestion to legislatures, I have provided a Model Statute in *Appendix C* as one possible way of drafting the rule.

The offer of judgment rule set out in the Model Statute should provide parties in litigation with a number of mechanisms to advance the potential for settlement. First, the value realized by a defendant in making an offer of judgment is greatest at the outset of the litigation and lessens over time. The value is greatest at that time because the bulk of the defendant's attorneys' fees have not yet been incurred and are potentially at risk for the plaintiff if the plaintiff declines the offer. This creates strong incentives for the defendant to consider with the greatest degree of deliberation and prudence the possibility that it might be liable, the likelihood the plaintiff will recover damages and its expected costs of defense if the litigation continues. These considerations are consistent with the civil justice goals of providing victims with fair compensation for their losses at the lowest transaction costs possible.

Second, while a certain level of gamesmanship and advocacy is inherent in any litigation context, the availability of an offer of judgment rule gives the defendant every incentive to make an offer that is as close as possible to the level that the plaintiff should reasonably hope to receive. The closer the defendant can come in directing its offer of judgment to the plaintiff's actual damages, the more likely it is that the plaintiff will accept the offer, thereby assisting the defendant with its goal of avoiding costs.

Third, although I have spoken about the offer of judgment rule as if it could only be applied by defendants against plaintiffs, the rule is actually neutral. As the Model Statute applies, it speaks to parties pursuing claims and parties defending claims, not plaintiffs and defendants. This means that in cases where both parties have claims against each other, whether the plaintiff in its complaint or the defendant in its counterclaim, the party defending against a claim will be able to use the offer of judgment rule as a tool to promote early settlement.

Fourth, unlike the current system in which irrational plaintiffs and foolish plaintiffs' lawyers are often rewarded for pursuing claims that have no merit, an offer of judgment rule takes away the leverage some claimants have as a result of the defendant's cost of defense. In the current system, a plaintiff can often extract a settlement that is derived from an estimation of the defendant's cost of defense. Through experience, plaintiffs' lawyers can become skilled at estimating what defendants will have to pay to defend against a claim. In those cases where the cost of defense dwarfs the actual damages at issue, skillful plaintiff's lawyers will try to persuade defendants that a settlement that works a discount from the defendant's inevitable cost of litigation is a net avoidance of cost for the defendant. In the current system it is quite ordinary for plaintiff's lawyers to shrug off any discussion of the weaknesses in their cases by pointing out that the defendant will have to pay more than the amount demanded simply to litigate the case.

With an offer of judgment rule, a plaintiff who pursues litigation and declines an offer of judgment that is an accurate estimate of its actual damages does so at great peril. In fact, to the extent that plaintiffs in the current system extract leverage from the defendant's cost of defense, the offer of judgment rule allows the defendant to gain some leverage from the difference between its cost of defense and the plaintiff's actual damages. By doing so, an offer of judgment rule punishes, rather than rewards, plaintiffs who pursue claims vindictively or for the purpose of "bleeding" the defendant through attorneys' fees when the plaintiff's actual damages are relatively slight.

Fifth, because the Model Statute speaks to offers on a claim and the attorneys' fees and costs associated with defending against that claim, it would be possible for parties to use an offer of judgment for some claims in a case but not all. This can be valuable for several reasons. For example, it is fairly common for plaintiff's attorneys in consumer and employment cases to couple statutory claims (such as those that provide for pro-plaintiff fee-shifting) with common law claims and claims for intentional torts (that contemplate punitive damages) in order to maximize the potential value of the overall case and in order to maximize the potential award for plaintiff's attorneys fees. While this tactic is understandable from the plaintiff's point of view (and effectively encouraged by the procedural rules that allow this tactic to continue) it makes no sense from an equitable point of view. The plaintiff can only claim to have been damaged once. Whether the claim was brought under a statute, under a common law tort or an intentional tort, the plaintiff has only suffered once and the plaintiff's actual damages do not grow with the number of theoretical causes of action that the plaintiff's attorney can glue together. By allowing the defendant to make an offer of judgment for a single claim, or for several claims on a claim-by-claim basis, the rule permits the defendant to force the plaintiff's attorney to truly consider the merits of his case.

For example, if a plaintiff has a meritworthy case for damages under Theory A, but a tenuous claim under Theory B, the defendant might offer the plaintiff only one dollar under Theory B. Doing that would force the plaintiff to consider whether it really had a viable claim under Theory B. If the plaintiff declined the offer and won its case under Theory A but lost under Theory B, the net outcome could be a wash or even a negative outcome for the plaintiff. Thus, one viable defense strategy with an offer of judgment rule like the Model Statute would be to make nominal offers on each of the plaintiff's weakest claims, thereby forcing the plaintiff to take a clearheaded look at each of its claims. In such a circumstance, the plaintiff might accept the one-dollar offer, dropping its frivolous claims and keeping only the meritworthy claim. All of this would advance the causes of equity and efficiency, however, by trimming the meritless claims out of the case.

This kind of thinking is not merely theoretical. From practical experience it is quite often that an adversary has a single viable claim but, in the hopes of winning the litigation lottery, has coupled the viable claim with any number of frivolous claims. The existence of the viable claim makes some judges reluctant to dismiss the entire matter or even to sanction the plaintiff or its counsel for persisting with the frivolous claims. Having the frivolous claims in the case can also work a strange psychological effect on the plaintiff and its counsel, causing them to pursue theories of discovery and lines of argument that are ultimately worthless but that increase the attorneys' fees on both sides of the case. Having a tool like an offer of judgment rule that forces a party soberly to consider the impact of pursuing frivolous claims, or pursuing claims beyond the value they are truly worth, will do much to force the early settlement of cases that ought to be settled.

Of course, defending parties will need to exercise care in making offers of judgment for less than the entire case. An offered judgment, when accepted, is a final judgment and can operate to establish certain facts between the parties. For example, in a case involving two causes of action under a single contract, if the defendant offered judgment on the first cause of action, the defendant would generally lose the ability, when defending against the second cause, to argue that there was no contract. But these kinds of tactical considerations do not detract from the larger goals served by the offer of judgment rule.

Sixth, and finally, an offer of judgment rule like the one found in the Model Statute is actually a very modest improvement to a rule that already exists in the federal system. In fact, attorneys reading this book should notice that Section 1 of the Model Statute is taken nearly verbatim from Rule 68 of the Federal Rules of Civil Procedure. The few variations from Rule 68 are significant, however.

Rule 68 already allows offers of judgment, but puts at risk only the offeror's costs from the point of offer onward. In practice, and as the courts have interpreted Rule 68, these costs can include court-imposed filing fees, the cost of photocopying documents, travel expenses, the fees paid to court reporters and similar expenses but not attorneys' fees. Thus, while Rule 68 can play a role in federal cases where there is substantial travel and documentary discovery, Rule 68 does not currently shift attorneys' fees, thereby leaving the defendant to bear the brunt of its transactional costs. The Model Statute adds the phrase "and reasonable attorneys fees" wherever the word "costs" appears in Rule 68.

The Model Statute also makes it clear that the party defending a claim can make an offer of judgment *on a particular claim* and that the offeree's risk of declining the offer rests in paying the offeror's attorneys' fees and costs associated with continuing the defense *of that particular claim*. The few words needed to make clear this concept in the Model Statute are absent in Rule 68 as presently written. For the reasons described above, to create a tool for winnowing out weak claims in a case that contains some strong claims, this concept of a claim-specific offer of judgment is helpful.

Finally, Section 2 of the Model Statute is new and does not relate to anything found in Rule 68 today. The purpose of Section 2 is to create standards for determining "reasonable attorneys' fees". One of the phenomena that is apparent from experience is that courts will often struggle to find exceptions to general rules to avoid harsh consequences for individual parties the court perceives to be sympathetic. Thus, as described earlier, where Rule 11 was intended to curb frivolous litigation by imposing sanctions on parties and their attorneys, in practice judges have gone to great lengths to stretch the bounds of Rule 11 to avoid actually imposing sanctions. In addition, even in those circumstances where judges have found parties to have violated Rule 11 by pursuing frivolous claims, some judges have avoided ordering the violators to pay the opposing party's attorneys' fees because of a perception that this outcome would be harsh.

If legislatures adopt an offer of judgment rule like the rule found in Section 1 of the Model Statute, it may be marginally better than the status quo but will be substantially less preferable to the outcome if Section 2 is included. Section 2 of the Model Statute outlines the factors the court should consider in awarding attorneys' fees and costs after an offeree declines an offer of judgment. The factors listed in Section 2 are largely consistent with the factors courts consider in other contexts in which one party is required to pay the other party's "reasonable attorneys' fees". Section 2 is different, however, because it mandates that, in a situation where the offeror has actually paid its attorney in cash, its "reasonable attorneys' fees" cannot be less than the amount it has already paid.

Some might worry that this last point, guaranteeing that the offeror recovers 100% of the attorneys' fees already paid in cash, would give defending parties too much incentive to "over-lawyer" a case. A defendant, the argument goes, would make a low ball offer to the plaintiff, expecting that it would be declined, and then proceed to hire the most expensive lawyers possible to exhaust every legal argument and stratagem available.

While there can be no guarantee that this would never happen (and, after all, there probably are some firms that already handle their cases this way) it is unlikely to pose a significant problem for the system at large. First, a defending party that is willing to pay exorbitant sums out of pocket to defend itself would be foolish to do so if it could settle the case for a small fraction of that amount. Over-lawyering only makes sense when the potential judgment is many times greater than the cost of defense. Second, the defending party could never have complete certainty that it would recover its exorbitant attorneys' fees. It would be taking a gamble. That gamble would be rational only if the cost of settlement was much higher than the cost of defense. Finally, a defending party who wanted to over-lawyer a case would be paying in cash for the privilege of doing so. While it might have a reason to do so in isolated situations, it would be extremely difficult to justify on a widespread basis.

Because opponents of reform often profess to fear the power of "big corporations," consider what would befall the "big corporation" that tried to over-lawyer all of its cases to take unfair advantage of an offer of judgment rule. It would, of course, regularly pay huge legal bills. Those legal bills would come out of the company's expenses and would impact its bottom line. For a publicly traded company, there is no upside to inflating expenses. Doing so would trade pain in the courtroom for pain in the boardroom and would be a losing strategy in the long run. Even if a corporate defendant felt confident that it could recover an award of attorneys' fees against a plaintiff, there could be no guarantee that it would be able to collect. If the plaintiff lacked the assets to satisfy the award, the defendant would still be left without reimbursement.

Moreover, imagine the public relations effects. If a large company ever tried to over-work all of its defense cases, watchdog organizations would bring the practice under public scrutiny. To the extent the company hoped to intimidate plaintiffs into a cheap settlement, the public relations effects could easily backfire, raising the costs of settlement. Even if the defending party were immune to public pressure, plaintiffs' attorneys could well expose the tactic to the court. No judge would want to preside over a proceeding that was grossly unfair and judges would use their bully pulpits to inveigh against any abuse.

In the long run, the most rational course for a defending party is to make an offer of judgment that is as close as possible to the plaintiff's likely recovery if the case were tried on the merits.

Guaranteeing the recovery of actual fees paid has additional benefits, however. In other contexts where a court must determine what attorneys' fees are reasonable, the court is often dealing with a plaintiff's attorney who is working under a contingent fee arrangement. That attorney may have little, if any, experience working for an hourly billable rate. Even if the attorney did have other clients who paid by the hour, it might not be reasonable to impute that billable rate to a case where the attorneys' fees are to be paid by the opposing party. Parties pay differently when they voluntarily undertake an hourly rate than when they are forced by the compulsion of law to pay an amount the court believes is reasonable. Because the purpose of the offer of judgment rule is to actually shift the burden of attorneys' fees from the party defending the claim to the party pursuing the claim, the only way that rule can work is if the shifting of fees at the end of the process is mandatory and free from any temptation to reduce the award because of sympathies or other factors.

Because the Model Statute is a variation on Federal Rule 68, it could be adopted by Congress as an amendment to Rule 68 or by a state legislature as a new provision in the state's rules of civil procedure. Some states already have analogs to Federal Rule 68 so the transition to the Model Statute would involve even less of a change.

The Model Statute does not address the relatively few cases where the special nature of the plaintiff requires some kind of exception. For example, in cases where the plaintiff is a government agency, in some class actions and in cases that seek only injunctive relief (and no money damages), the offer of judgment rule may require special exceptions. These exceptions can take a variety of forms, however, from prohibiting offers of judgment altogether to limiting the amount or percentage of attorneys' fees that an offeror may recover.[119] Because these special cases are a very small percentage of the overall litigation burden and should not detract from the greater value of reducing transaction costs, I have not tried to suggest a uniform solution in the Model Rule.

It is this aspect that I think holds the most promise for substantially changing the way parties approach the business of litigation in America. The bulk of the impact of American litigation is the over $170 billion in excess transaction costs pushed through the system every year. That figure, which is derived from 2002 data, is growing every year and consumes a sizeable percentage of our economy. Other reforms may be more appealing to particular interest groups. Stories that occupy the attention of the media from time to time may suggest a "crisis" in one industry or another, but these anecdotal glimpses of the crushing impact of litigation are small pieces of a much larger puzzle. Putting together that larger puzzle into a system that solves the problem of litigation transaction costs requires a reform that is at once modest and at the same time far-reaching in its implications.

By adopting an offer of judgment rule that adds only a few words to existing federal law, reform along these lines is politically streamlined. As reforms go, this one is small. Simultaneously, however, by giving parties who are victimized by litigation the ability to shift the burden of defending themselves onto the parties who initiate litigation, this reform does more than any other to change the business of litigation in America for the better.

Offer of Judgment Rules in the States

What makes an offer of judgment rule like the one in the Model Statute appealing is that this experiment has already been tried in a handful of states. With the benefit of experience in those states, this kind of reform has the appearance of an improvement on the rules rather than a radical departure.

Four states in particular—Alaska, Oklahoma, Florida and Texas—have adopted offer of judgment rules that, in varying degrees and in surprisingly different ways—work to shift fees when one party offers to settle but the offer is declined. The way that these rules work in these states will be helpful in understanding why my proposed Model Statute works the way it does.

---

119. *Compare* Texas Civ. Prac. and Rem. Code §§ 42.002(a)-(b) (2003). (excluding the Texas offer of judgment rule in class actions, shareholder derivative suits, governmental actions, child custody and divorce actions, actions to collect workers' compensation benefits, small claims cases and cases for injunctive relief) *with* Fla. Rules of Civ. P., 773 So. 2d 1098, 1119 (Fla. 2000) (amending Rule 1.442 to allow named plaintiffs in a putative class action until thirty days after the certification or denial of class status to accept or reject a proposed offer of judgment, effective January 1, 2001), *but see also, Betts v. Ace Cash Express, Inc.*, 863 S.E.2d 1252 (Fla. App. Jan. 2., 2004) (affirming trial court ruling that named plaintiffs were liable for defendant's attorneys' fees of $63,483 when named plaintiffs' rejected settlement offer under offer of judgment rule prior to the effective date of the amendment to Rule 1.442).

It is fair to note, however, that two states also have a very different kind of fee-shifting and I am not focusing on the experiences in those states under those rules. California has a number of statutes that allow parties in certain kinds of cases to recover their attorneys' fees, but most of these statutes leave the award to the discretion of the court (meaning that there can be no guarantee that the winner will recover its attorneys' fees) and most of the statutes, in practice, only award fees to a prevailing plaintiff.[120] In addition, although Texas adopted a fee-shifting offer of judgment rule in 2003, it also has a much older law that contemplates fee-shifting in certain kinds of suits involving payment for services rendered and on certain kinds of contracts.[121] The older Texas rule, however, is limited to fairly narrow kinds of contractual claims and does not apply to contracts generally or to tort claims. Consequently neither of these rules is a good example of the kind of comprehensive, fee-shifting offer of judgment rule approach prescribed by the Model Statute.

Offer of Judgment in Alaska

Alaska is in the unique situation of having both a loser-pays rule that automatically awards some attorneys' fees to the prevailing party as well as an offer of judgment rule that provides for additional fee-shifting.

Alaska's loser-pays rule, however, is somewhat diluted. Currently, a defendant who prevails by avoiding any liability can recover no more than 30% of its actual attorneys' fees. Prior to 1993, the Alaska loser-pays rule provided for a greater percentage of automatic attorneys' fees for the prevailing party, but the automatic amount was reduced in 1993 as part of a reform effort. In 1997, Alaska modified its offer of judgment rule, to allow parties to shift attorneys' fees. Prior to 1997, Rule 68 of the Alaska Rules of Civil Procedure mirrored Federal Rule 68,[122] allowing a party defending a claim to make an offer of settlement. If the offer was declined and the offering party subsequently prevailed or was found liable for less than the amount of the offer, the party declining the settlement offer was obligated to reimburse the offering party its "costs". For cases filed on or after August

---

120. Lorraine Wright Feuerstein, *Two-Way Fee Shifting on Summary Judgment or Dismissal, supra* n68 at 155.
121. *Id.* at 152.
122. Alaska R. Civ. P. 68, *available at* http://www.state.ak.us/courts/civ2.htm#82. Alaska's "old" Rule 68 applies to cases filed before August 7, 1997 and the new rule applies to cases filed on or after that date.

7, 1997, Alaska's "new" Rule 68 provides that the offering party's attorneys' fees as well as costs may shift to the party declining the settlement offer.

Alaska's new Rule 68, however, limits the percentage of attorneys' fees that the offering party can recover and sets thresholds by which to compare the claiming party's actual judgment against the judgment offered by the defending party. If the offer of judgment was made in the early discovery portion of litigation, the offer of judgment may shift as much as 75% of the offeror's reasonable actual attorneys' fees. An offer made after that point, but at least 90 days before trial may shift as much as 50% of the offeror's reasonable actual attorneys' fees, while an offer made after that point, but at least 10 days before trial may shift only 30% of the offeror's fees.[123] In any of these situations, the offeror will recover attorneys' fees only if it prevails or if the judgment against it is at least 5% less than the amount of the offer. A recovery inside of the 5% threshold will leave each party bearing its own fees.

Read in tandem with Alaska's loser-pays rule (Alaska Rule 82), these numbers have a certain symmetry, with a prevailing party who is defending a claim (but making no offer of judgment) entitled to between 20% and 30% of its actual attorneys' fees if it prevails and with a party having the chance to recover greater percentages, from 30% to 75%, if it makes an offer of judgment. The earlier in the proceedings the offer of judgment is made, the greater percentage of attorneys' fees is "in play" and potentially at risk for the claimant.

Offer of Judgment in Florida

Florida's version of the offer of judgment rule also has some unique elements. Under the Florida rule, the party defending against a claim may make a settlement offer and the opposing party has thirty days in which to accept or reject the offer.[124] If the offeror prevails or suffers a judgment that at least 25% less than the offer, then the offeror can recover all of its actual attorneys' fees and expenses. At the same time, a party who is pursuing a claim can make an offer of judgment to the defending party under the same rule. If the party making the claim receives a judgment that exceeds the amount of the offer by at least 25% it will also be entitled to collect its actual attorneys' fees from the defending party.

Unlike Alaska's offer of judgment rule, the Florida statute puts no percentage limits on the amount of attorneys' fees a prevailing offeror can recover. The Flor-

---

123. Alaska R. Civ. P. 68.
124. Fla. Stat. 786.79.

ida statute also uses a 25% threshold to qualify for fee-shifting as opposed to the 5% threshold in Alaska. In addition, unlike the rule in Alaska, the Florida rule allows either the claimant or the defending party to make an offer and thereby put its attorneys' fees in play. By doing so, the Florida rule avoids the criticism that it is preliminary of benefit to defendants. Like the pure English rule, the Florida offer of judgment rule not only deters frivolous cases by potentially imposing defendants' attorneys' fees on plaintiffs but also deters dilatory tactics by defendants when the plaintiff has been sufficiently savvy to make an offer of judgment that is in the ballpark of its likely recovery.

Offer of Judgment in Oklahoma

Oklahoma first adopted a version of the offer of judgment rule in 1995.[125] The provision began as part of an overall litigation reform package but was diluted under pressure from a variety of interest groups. The final version of the rule applied only to personal injury cases in which the plaintiff sought, or the plaintiff offered a judgment, of $100,000 or more.[126] It permitted the defendant in a personal injury case to shift fees through an offer of judgment and permitted the plaintiff who received an offer of judgment to make a counteroffer as well.

The Oklahoma legislature amended the rule twice thereafter, in 1999 and 2002, expanding the rule to include all civil cases.[127] Under the version of the rule now in effect, a defendant can shift its attorneys' fees through an offer of judgment and a plaintiff may also shift its attorneys' fees through a counteroffer. Unlike the Florida and Alaska rules, the Oklahoma rule does not provide for a threshold that must be surpassed before fees are shifted. If either party declines a settlement offer and the final judgment is less favorable than the declined offer, the offeree can be required to pay the offeror's attorneys' fees.

Offer of Judgment in Texas

As part of a comprehensive litigation reform package in 2003, Texas also adopted an offer of judgment rule.[128] The Texas offer of judgment rule allows defendants to file a declaration that puts the rule into effect in a pending case. Once the defendant files the declaration, either the plaintiff or the defendant may make a settlement offer. If the offer is rejected and the resulting judgment is less favor-

---

125. Olson and Bernstein, *Loser-Pays, supra* n36 at 1175-1176.
126. *Id.*
127. Okla. Stat. 12-1101.1.

able to the party declining the offer by a factor of twenty percent, then the party who rejected the settlement offer is responsible for the offering party's "litigation costs", defined to include court costs, the fees of up to two expert witnesses and reasonable attorneys' fees.[129]

The State Experience Overall

As with much when it comes to litigation reform, there is little data available to assess how effective offer of judgment rules have been at reducing the incidence of litigation. It is noteworthy, however, that among the 49 jurisdictions reporting to the National Center for State Courts data regarding the number of cases filed per capita that Florida ranked 19th and Alaska ranked 34th in total civil cases filed in 2002.[130] More encouraging, however, is the rate at which civil case filings have grown (or declined) in various states over the decade from 1993 to 2002. In Alaska, the rate of tort cases filed has grown by 7% during this period (noting that it was in 1993 that Alaska relaxed its loser-pays rule to benefit plaintiffs). In Florida, the rate of tort cases filed fell by 25%.[131] Of the 31 jurisdictions reporting the rate of tort filings during this period only 8 had a decline greater than the decline in Florida. During the same period, of the 25 states reporting the rate of contract case filings, Florida and Alaska were 2nd and 3rd, respectively, in decreasing the number of cases filed.[132]

Part of the thesis behind the offer of judgment rule, however, is that it should not only deter weak cases from being filed but should also encourage the speedy settlement of weak cases and those where liability is clear. On that score the evidence is pronounced. Among 21 jurisdictions reporting the disposition rates of

---

128. Texas H.B. 78 (2003 Sess.; effective Sept 1, 2003), *available at* http://www. capitol.state.tx.us/cgi-bin/db2www/tlo/billhist/billhist.d2w/report? HISTORY=Basic&LEG=78&SESS=R&CHAMBER=H&BILLTYPE=B& BILLSUFFIX=00004

129. *Id.* at § 2.01.

130. National Center for State Courts, *Examining the Work of State Courts 2003, supra* n5 at 20. Unfortunately, Oklahoma did not report this data to NCSC for 2002. Florida had 5,878 cases and Alaska had 4,149 cases per 100,000 in population. The District of Columbia, Maryland and Virginia lead the list with over 14,000 cases per 100,000 and Tennessee was the lowest-filing jurisdiction with only 1,167 cases per 100,000. Oklahoma did not report its results to the NCSC and, because the Texas offer of judgment rule took effect only a little more than one year ago, there is no comprehensive data available on its effect in Texas.

131. *Id.* at 24.

civil cases (i.e., the percentage of cases filed that proceed to trial versus those that are resolved at an earlier stage), Florida and Alaska are the 2nd and 9th most efficient jurisdictions, respectively.[133] In Florida, 98.6% of all cases are resolved before trial. In Alaska, 96.1% of all cases are resolved before trial. These disposition rates compare well to the average disposition rate of 92.4%.[134]

While this statistical evidence is not scientific and does not necessarily link the changes in rate of case filings and dispositions to the offer of judgment rules, it is suggestive. Clearly Alaska and Florida, which have offer of judgment rules, are among the most efficient jurisdictions in the nation at resolving cases prior to trial. Florida, with its offer of judgment rule, experienced a declining rate of tort and contract case filings over a ten-year period. This suggests that an offer of judgment rule may be effective at reducing the incidence and duration of civil suits. The fact that three states have experimented with various offer of judgment rules shows that the measure can be popular with legislators. The experience in Alaska, which has had a form of loser-pays for more than 100 years and in Oklahoma, which adopted a narrow fee-shifting rule in 1995 only to expand it a few years later, demonstrate that the provision can survive and even grow in popularity over time.

---

132. *Id.* Filings in Alaska declined by 26% over the decade while filings in Florida declined by 28%. Only Maine reduced its rate of contract filings by a greater amount. Oklahoma did not report its results. Because judicial reporting to the NCSC is voluntary, the number of states reporting tort filings differs from the number reporting contract case filings.

133. *Id.* at 22.

134. *Id.* The only jurisdiction with a higher disposition rate than Florida is the District of Columbia at 99.2%. The District of Columbia, however, is also the jurisdiction with the highest rate of civil cases filings for its population (nearly three times the per capita frequency of case filings in Florida), suggesting that both the filing rate and the disposition rate in the District of Columbia may be atypical.

8

Alternative Reforms

People obviously have the ability to go to court. But by what rules and standards? Our modern consciousness is so focused on individual rights that we can't conceive of another way to ensure fairness. But if lawsuits are recognized as an exercise of state power, perhaps the state should make conscious judgments of who can sue for what. That's what legal rules and interpretations are for. Philip K. Howard, THE COLLAPSE OF THE COMMON GOOD (2001).

I have proposed two types of reforms I believe will be effective at reducing the number of lawsuits filed every year and reducing the transactions costs of those lawsuits. By limiting punitive damages to the amounts the Supreme Court has ruled are constitutionally permissible, Congress and the legislatures will reduce some of the incentives for plaintiffs and their lawyers to file lawsuits that have the primary purpose of pursuing a recovery of punitive damages. By adopting a mechanism for shifting attorneys' fees when a defendant makes an offer of judgment, parties who are pursuing claims will have to consider carefully whether their claims are worth the possible risk of having to pay the opposing party's attorneys.

Litigation reform is nothing new, however. For the past two decades some writers have warned of a "crisis" in the American litigation system. Groups like the American Tort Reform Association have written papers and tried to educate the public on the cost of litigation and have proposed a variety of reform solutions. Why haven't these efforts borne more fruit?

Why haven't the reforms that have been adopted been more effective at reducing litigation? After all, 34 of the fifty states adopted limitations on punitive damages and 31 of those laws survived constitutional challenge in their states. Although 26 of those 31 states still permitted plaintiffs to recover punitive damages that were double or greater the award of compensatory damages, those limitations must have dampened incentives for plaintiffs to some extent. If so, why do so many advocates for reform still perceive that litigation is increasing? Why did the direct costs of tort litigation increase 14.4% in 2001 and 13.3% in 2002?[135] Why is the civil litigation system still in crisis?

Some writers believe that the pace of litigation is slowing somewhat and have written about reform efforts in individual states, attempting to show how reforms have made headway. As before, however, quantifying the impact of formal changes in the law on the incidence and cost of litigation is so difficult as to defy solution. Capping punitive damages in one state might simply lead the plaintiff to file a claim in a state where there is no cap. Without the kind of detailed and comprehensive data collection and reporting that simply doesn't exist today, it will probably always be impossible to quantify exactly which reforms are effective and by how much.

Nevertheless, the lack of empirical data should not pose an insurmountable challenge to the efforts of reform. Even if we cannot quantify every dollar's worth of change from one reform or another, we should not abandon common sense. From this point of view, I would like to discuss a few alternative reforms that some have proposed and consider their merits in comparison to the reforms I have proposed.

Reforms Specific to Medical Malpractice

Medical malpractice and the crisis in American healthcare have driven much of the debate over litigation reform in the past few years. It isn't hard to see why. Healthcare touches everyone in a very personal way. Healthcare often involves life and death issues. Decisions made by a surgeon on the operating table can easily end a life or change it dramatically. That potential for life-changing impacts makes doctors and healthcare providers prime targets for litigation when a medical procedure has a negative result.

Medical litigation also has the potential to generate headlines in a way that business litigation does not. The evening news magazine television shows every week feature dramatic medical stories involving strange illnesses, high-risk pregnancies and childhood surgeries. These stories are dramatic and draw upon some of the most emotional material that parents can imagine. In those situations where something goes wrong—a baby dies, a father is disabled, a child suffers a debilitating injury that will last for the rest of its life—the story is gripping and

---

135. Tillinghast-Towers Perrin, *supra* n6 at 1.

the patient is sympathetic. The audience wants to understand what went wrong. If a plaintiffs' lawyer can put that story in front of a jury and suggest that the doctor, the hospital or the insurance company stood in the way of a better outcome, it can be extremely difficult to persuade the jury that imposing liability on that doctor, hospital or insurance company is the wrong solution.

In recent years, rising rates for medical malpractice insurance have not only increased the rates paid by most Americans for health insurance but have even made certain high-risk medical specialties difficult to find in some jurisdictions. In several states, for example, Obstetricians are becoming scarce.[136] This leaves pregnant women without easy access to Ob/Gyn services, in some cases requiring pregnant women to travel great distances (even into adjoining states) in order to find medical care for their pregnancies.

This focus on medical malpractice has prompted some to suggest reforms aimed only at medical malpractice cases. Some have suggested special courts that would hear only medical cases. The judges in these courts would receive special training or have access to independent experts who would give the court independent guidance on the medical and scientific issues present in medical malpractice cases.

Others, including President Bush and some in the Kerry/Edwards 2004 campaign, suggested that legislatures should adopt special pre-screening procedures that would require potential plaintiffs to have their cases reviewed by boards of independent experts. Plaintiffs would be prohibited from filing suit unless the pre-screening board determined the case had merit.

While reforms like this might make sense in some jurisdictions where the medical malpractice crisis is particularly acute, these kinds of reforms are unlikely to create a more efficient litigation system in the long run and will do nothing to stem the tide of litigation outside the narrow area of medical malpractice.

Pre-screening solutions necessarily involve significant changes to the law. Reform legislation would have to define which cases would be subject to the pre-screening requirements and which would not. The legislation would have to cre-

---

136. Christopher Guadagnino, *Obstetrician Scarcity in Pennsylvania*, Physician's News Digest (2004) *available at* http://www.physiciansnews.com/cover/504.html ("Quantifying the severity of physician scarcity in Pa. is notoriously difficult. Using data from the U.S. Bureau of Health Professions and the American Medical Association, the Pennsylvania Medical Society notes that Pa. lost 40 obstetricians between 2000 to 2002, the most recent data available. Regarding young physicians, Pa. ranked 41st among states in 2000 for its percentage of physicians under age 35, a sharp decline from its 12th-place spot in 1989.").

ate a system of pre-screening boards, staffing the boards with independent experts, developing standards for the experts to apply in screening cases, and determining standards of review and evaluation. Because the pre-screening boards would effectively deny potential plaintiffs the right to sue if their cases fell below some threshold of viability, such legislation would almost certainly come under constitutional attack.

The entire process of medical malpractice reform would encounter resistance every step of the way. Who would choose the independent experts who would sit on the screening boards? How would those experts be paid? Would experts be permitted to have other employment or would they be full-time employees of the state? If experts had other employment, what conflict of interest rules would the experts need to follow to ensure that their opinions would be unbiased? Examining the composition of the expert boards and the selection of expert panelists could easily devolve into a political quagmire that would threaten the feasibility of the entire system.

How would the experts differentiate the viable cases from the frivolous ones? Would the experts reject every case that they believed would ultimately fail to prove liability or would they reject only those cases that were so frivolous that there was no set of circumstances under which the plaintiff might prevail? If the threshold for approval was too high, the screening system might preclude merit-worthy cases from ever reaching the courtroom. That outcome would not only be unfair to injured patients but would impinge their constitutional right to access to the courts. If the threshold was too low—screening out only those cases where the facts could never amount to a plaintiff's victory—the screening process would have no benefit, since nearly every proposed case would get passed on to the courts. In fact, a screening process with an overly low threshold might even make malpractice litigation worse, since every complaint that made it to court would have the implied "blessing" of the pre-screening board.

Would the potential defendant have the opportunity to be heard by the pre-screening board or would the board consider only the plaintiff's claims? If the defendant had the chance to provide evidence to the screening board, what rules of evidence would apply? Who would rule on the admissibility of evidence and could those rulings be appealed? Would the plaintiff and the defendant have the ability to call witnesses and present evidence, or would the screening board consider the case in a vacuum? Once you stop to think through all of the minute details a pre-screening system would entail, it becomes clear that this kind of reform would not be efficient and might even cost more and create more litigation than the status quo.

By requiring the implementation of a screening program, reformers would have to justify all of the details of the plan in the legislative process and in the attendant public relations efforts. The opponents of reform would be able to attack not only the larger concept but also every detail of the legislation. Assuming that a legislature passed a pre-screening bill, the new law would also be attacked on constitutional grounds in the courts. The complexity of the reform would increase the number and types of constitutional arguments its opponents would have.

To the extent that the pre-screening reform merely shifted *when* the litigants would make the arguments they would ordinarily make at the preliminary motion and summary judgment stages of litigation, it would really have no impact. Both plaintiff and defendant would have to raise and brief these potentially dispositive arguments. Doing so would still require all of the affected parties to hire and pay lawyers to make those arguments. The process through pre-screening and into the courts might take longer, but it would seem inevitably to involve substantially the same arguments as in the current system. While the outcomes might change because of the medical and scientific contributions of the experts on the screening boards, the reform would be so complicated that it is hard to see how it would make the overall system more efficient.

Collateral Source Rule

Another reform that some have suggested relates to the kind of evidence jurors may hear when considering allocating damages to a single defendant. Called the "collateral source rule', it prohibits a defendant from telling the jury that the plaintiff has recovered money from other sources in connection with the injury for which the plaintiff is suing the defendant. In theory, the collateral source rule gives the plaintiff the opportunity to have a double (or even greater) recovery by suing several defendants in separate actions over the same injury.[137]

For example, consider a patient who has an appendectomy performed by a surgeon. During the surgery a series of mishaps result in damage to one of the patient's other organs. As a result, the patient requires continuing medical care and medicines to treat the injured organ for the rest of his life. Assume that the patient's new doctors estimate that the cost of the patient's medical care and drugs for the rest of his life will cost $100,000. Under the collateral source rule the patient could sue the surgeon for negligence in performing the surgery, the

---

137. *See, e.g.*, http://www.atra.org/show/7344.

hospital for negligently permitting the surgeon to perform the surgery and other parties who may have been involved in the procedure in separate cases. In each one of those several cases the patient would point to his lifetime future expense of $100,000 as his compensatory damages. The patient would probably try to recover punitive damages as well. Under the collateral source rule, the patient could recover $100,000 from the surgeon and the hospital (and anyone else he might be able to identify with a cause of action) and collect his projected lifetime expenses several times over. In each of those cases, the surgeon would be prohibited from telling the jury that the patient had also sued the hospital and the hospital would likewise be unable to talk about the patient's recovery from the surgeon.

Reforming the collateral source rule makes sense. If the purpose of civil justice is to compensate victims for their injuries it is not well served by allowing victims to recover more than what their injuries are worth. A double recovery represents a windfall to the plaintiff at a cost to society. One source suggests that up to 35% of total payments made in medical malpractice cases are for costs that have already been paid by other sources.[138] In addition, by proliferating cases for the same set of circumstances, the collateral source rule increases the inefficiency of litigation.

As of July 2004, twenty-three states have adopted some kind of reform of the collateral source rule or have eliminated it altogether.[139] While reforming this area of the law would probably improve the equity of the litigation system overall, on balance it would probably have a less immediate effect than fee-shifting rules and caps on punitive damages.

The collateral source rule only comes into play where the plaintiff has the opportunity to recover from several defendants or where the plaintiff has already been compensated (perhaps from insurance) but wants to assert claims against an additional source. While reforming the collateral source rule may be an important reform that will work substantial justice in certain cases, it probably will not contribute a significant amount towards the overall burden of excessive litigation.

Class Action Limitations

Many advocates of reform point to the role of class actions in generating huge costs. They point to the many cases where class actions have resulted in minimal

---

138. American Tort Reform Association, *Tort Reform Record*, 13 (July 13, 2004).
139. *Id.*

recoveries to class members but have generated substantial fee awards for the plaintiffs' attorneys. Some of the most notorious "blockbuster" awards of punitive damages have come in class action cases and they have come to symbolize much of the abuse in the current system.

Traditionally, the class action mechanism has two purposes: one for the benefit of plaintiffs and another for the benefit of defendants. The class action mechanism allows similarly situated plaintiffs to band together to share costs and risks in situations where their individual claims, taken singly, might not make litigation worthwhile but where all of their claims, taken together, make for a significant amount at issue. The class action mechanism originated from an ancient English remedy called the "bill of peace" which allowed a single defendant to resolve the claims of many similar plaintiffs by offering a comprehensive remedy to all of them. In its current form, class actions in the federal courts under Federal Rule 23 and in the states under analogous provisions, theoretically give defendants the ability to reduce their costs by grouping a large number of plaintiffs into a class that can be managed through a single, consolidated class remedy.

In practice, however, modern class actions rarely work for the defendant as did the ancient "bill of peace". In contrast, most current class actions are generated by plaintiffs' attorneys who scan the headlines for developments involving large corporations that could theoretically lead to a large number of potential plaintiffs. These plaintiffs' lawyers may never even meet their putative clients, and the class action complaints are usually filed with only one or a small handful of actual plaintiffs involved. The vast majority of the putative class members may have no knowledge that they have a claim or even that they are part of a class. In some cases, if asked, putative class members would not have chosen to be a part of the case.[140] In short, the original rationale of helping plaintiffs to "band together" no longer plays a role in class actions that are driven almost entirely by attorneys who make a business of creating these lawsuits.

Another recent phenomenon with class action lawsuits is the rise in cases where plaintiffs' lawyers will bring a putative class suit against all of the members in an entire industry, or against the leaders in that industry, not to claim any particular money damages but rather to achieve some kind of public policy goal

---

140. I am aware of at least one lawsuit where two of the three named plaintiffs were unaware of their claims until more than two years after the complaint was filed, when they were invited to become representative members of the class by the plaintiffs' attorney. In that same case, five putative class members came forward to testify that they didn't believe the case was justified and would not have taken part in it if they had a choice.

(whether reducing greenhouse gasses, changing the way the industry bills its customers or some other non-monetary change). By seeking a change in practice—rather than a sum of money—the plaintiffs' lawyers try to "take the high road" by claiming to work for the public good. Of course in the inevitable settlement discussions that follow in such cases the plaintiffs' attorneys always demand that the defendants pay their fees.

These kinds of putative class actions in many instances are little more than disguised shakedown operations with plaintiffs' lawyers claiming to be working on behalf of the public only to demand payment of their fees later. Moreover, to the extent that regulating industry is properly the role of the legislature, permitting private attorneys to file their own lawsuits in pursuit of what they claim is the "public good" is a recipe for disaster in the regulatory arena.[141] Private attorneys represent only their clients and not the public at large. They are unelected and accountable only to their private clients. They have no special knowledge or skills that qualify them to speak on behalf of the public and are immune from public criticism if their perception of the public good is inaccurate. Regulation through litigation, at its best, merely usurps the legislature's proper role. At worst, it becomes a fourth estate, making law outside of the checks and balances that properly restrain the three branches of government.

The difficulty in tackling the class action problem, however, is in the unintended effects of possible solutions. Eliminating class actions altogether would solve the problem but would leave defendants without the ability to get a comprehensive solution in those few cases where one is needed. That cure could be worse than the disease.

Another solution is federalizing the class action problem by requiring all class actions above a certain threshold to be filed in federal courts. By moving all large class actions into federal court, litigants would benefit by the more-developed federal procedural laws and the greater consistencies that exist in the federal trial courts. This would, however, increase the need for additional federal judges and other resources to handle the heavier caseload and would also raise some unique constitutional problems. Federal courts only have jurisdiction over cases that involve questions of federal law or where the plaintiff and defendant are residents of different states.[142] This limitation on federal court jurisdiction is established in

---

141. *See, e.g.*, Panel Discussion, *The New Class Action Targets: Are Class Actions Undermining Regulation in the Fields of Financial Services, High Technology and Telecommunications?* (Center for Legal Policy at the Manhattan Institute, October 30, 2002) *available at* http://www.fed-soc.org/Publications/Transcripts/classactions1.pdf.

142. *See* Chapter 2 for a discussion of federal court jurisdiction.

Article III of the U.S. Constitution and cannot be changed by Congressional legislation. As a result, federalizing class actions will only survive constitutional challenge if reformers can find a way to push the reform through the very narrow constitutional window that establishes federal court jurisdiction.

One example of this approach was the Class Action Fairness Act of 2003.[143] Although this bill never became law, it passed the House by a vote of 253-170 in June 2003 and missed passage in the Senate by one vote a few months thereafter.[144] Looking at the history of this bill helps in understanding why reforming the class action rules can be so difficult.

The Class Action Fairness Act was first introduced in the 105th Congress in 1997 and has been resurrected several times since then.[145] The Class Action Fairness Act was intended to address a number of abuses involving class actions, including forum-shopping on the part of plaintiffs' lawyers, a loophole in the rules involving diversity jurisdiction that plaintiffs' lawyers use to keep their cases in friendly state courts instead of the more rigorous federal courts and the abuse of the class action procedure by plaintiffs in "mass tort" cases to extort settlements through the mere potential of massive liability.

While limiting the ability of plaintiffs' lawyers to "shop" for the most favorable state jurisdiction and tightening rules to keep truly national cases in federal court may help keep some class actions under control, it is hard to imagine that tinkering in the margins with these kinds of procedural rules will really cause significant change to the overall system. Class actions are on the rise, but account for only a small fraction of the estimated 6 million torts and contracts cases filed in state courts in 2002. The class action rules merit reform, but reforming this aspect of the litigation system will not be enough, by itself, to really change the big picture.

Another alternative method of reforming the class action rules would be to limit the availability of "opt-out" classes (those where every theoretical member of a class is part of the case unless that member affirmative decides not to take part, by completing a court-prescribed form and mailing it in). This kind of solution has promise because it strikes at the heart of the problem of lawyer-driven class actions. In the current system, plaintiffs' lawyers can claim to represent

---

143. Class Action Fairness Act, H.R. 1115, 108th Cong., 2003, and S. 274, 108th Cong. (2004).

144. *See* Report of the Senate Judiciary Committee on S.B. 274, 108. Cong. 123, *available at* http://thomas.loc.gov/cgi-bin/cpquery/T?&report = sr123&dbname=cp108&.

145. Senate Report 108-123, *supra* n40.

classes of thousands of potential plaintiffs merely because one member of that class has signed a representation agreement with the lawyer and that lawyer drafted the complaint as a class action. No other class member has consented to the lawyer's involvement. The lawyer has simply presumed himself to act on behalf of the class. If there were no class actions except where individual class members completed and mailed a form that indicated their willingness to be part of the lawsuit, it seems likely that there would be fewer classes and fewer class members.

One potential problem with eliminating or reducing opt-out class litigation is the role of the defensive class action. It is the heart of the opt-out class rule that allows defendants in some cases to ensure a comprehensive solution to a mass tort problem. If all class actions were opt-in classes, some defendants might be faced with multiple opt-in classes over the same subject matter in different courts. It might even be possible for the same individual plaintiffs to be members of more than one opt-in class for the same alleged injury.

While the class action rules need reform, I have not yet seen a proposal for reforming class litigation that entirely serves the needs of fairness for both plaintiffs and defendants. Even if I could find such a reform, the difficulty in generating political momentum around this issue would be difficult. It is hard enough to explain to voters how the cost of litigation affects them personally. Reforming the arcane rules of class litigation would certainly be even more difficult.

Limitations on Contingent Fees

Many reformers have focused on limiting litigation through changing the rules governing contingent fees. This approach has also proven emotional as the American approach to contingent fees is a byproduct of the Progressive Era and summons arguments regarding equal access to the courts. Plaintiffs' organizations in particular have reacted emotionally and have taken offense to discussions about reforming the contingent fee rules.

In a contingent fee arrangement the plaintiff's lawyer bargains with the plaintiff to get paid based upon a percentage of eventual recovery. Percentage recoveries generally range from 10% to 40% or more. The attorney's fee can vary, based upon the size of the recovery or the stage of the litigation in which the recovery is made, giving the attorney a smaller percentage if the case settles quickly or a higher percentage if the case goes all the way to trial. The merit of the contingent fee arrangement is that it allows a plaintiff to hire an attorney without actually spending any money. This permits plaintiffs with little income or resources to hire an attorney to pursue a claim. Without the contingent fee option, those plaintiffs might not have access to the courts.

Contingent fees should also, in theory, act as a screening mechanism to prevent frivolous cases from being filed. If the plaintiff's attorney is paid by the hour (the argument goes) the attorney has little incentive to weed out the weaker cases from the stronger ones. As long as his fees are paid he has no reason to care if his cases win or lose.

Contingent fees are a unique element in the American litigation system. Contingent fees are very rare in England and in most other industrialized countries. Critics have sometimes pointed to this fact as evidence that the American contingent fee system promotes litigation. That argument suggests that by converting attorneys from paid advocates for a party to a stakeholder in the outcome, the contingent fee distorts the professional incentives of lawyers, inducing them to pursue cases for the purpose of generating legal fees when the merits of those cases would suggest settlement.

There is some support for this view, especially in the context of class actions for money damages. As we have seen, under the current system there is little risk that a plaintiff will ever have to reimburse a defendant if the plaintiff's case is dismissed. Coupling that fact with the availability of contingent fees allows plaintiffs to pursue claims without a downside. An enterprising plaintiff's attorney can quickly build up a stable of pending contingent fee cases, filing as many as he can manage without much regard for their merit. Even if the vast majority of those cases ultimately lose or are abandoned, generating a settlement in even a small fraction of the cases can be sufficient to generate a nice living for the attorney. While the career plaintiff's attorney will probably take a case to trial every now and then, simply to maintain his *bona fides* as a fearsome trial lawyer, it will be rare that the attorney must expend his energies into trial as he will try to settle cases earlier in the process to maximize his own income.

While it is fairly easy to find fault with this system, which treats the litigation process like a lottery, it is less easy to reform it. Lawyer's contingency fees, to the extent they are subject to any regulation at all, are regulated at the state level. In some states they are the subject of ethical canons maintained by the state's bar. In some states they are limited by statute. Consequently, any limitation on contingent fees will need to be adopted at the state level and reform legislation will need to account for changes in lawyer's rules of professional ethics and the interplay of the legislation with those ethical rules.

Prohibiting contingent fees would reduce litigation by forcing a large number of plaintiffs out of the litigation system. This draconian approach, however, would probably force too many cases out of the system, as a large number of plaintiffs require the contingent fee mechanism to be able to afford counsel. Reducing litigation by pricing all plaintiffs out of the courts would not serve the equity goals of the litigation system and would be rightly attacked by consumer groups as well as plaintiffs' lawyers.

But how else could policy makers reform the rules for contingent fees without abolishing them entirely? Capping them at some fixed percentage is problematic because what might be a generous percentage in one case may be insufficient in another. It is difficult to find the "true" price of a plaintiffs' attorney's services because there is no real market for those services. A market for apples sets prices based upon consumers' need for apples and their abundance (supply) in the market. Through the interplay of supply and demand the market sets a price that works, more or less, for consumer and producers.

No such market exists for plaintiffs' attorneys because:

a. Each individual case is different, presenting unique potential rewards against the potential wasted effort if the case loses. Different plaintiffs' attorneys may value the same case very differently based on their perception of its value and the risk of loss.

b. Purchasers cannot differentiate among the sources of supply. The purchasers of attorney services (i.e., the potential plaintiffs) usually cannot differentiate between the features and benefits of competing attorneys. The average non-lawyer is unable to tell whether Attorney A is better than Attorney B or vice versa. In the apple marketplace, except for variations between different varieties of apples (which are understood by people who eat apples) and variations in quality (which are apparent by looking at them) all apples are the same.

c. There are high barriers to information in this market. To find out whether Attorney A will take a case the plaintiff must seek out the attorney, provide the attorney with background information, answer any questions and then ask the attorney if he would be willing to take the case and, if so, for how much. To get a second opinion on price, the individual plaintiff must seek out a second attorney and go through the entire consultation process again. Because this process takes time and effort a potential plaintiff is unable to determine what the "true" market price for the attorney's services will be. (In the market for apples, the consumer can look up prices in a newspaper or telephone several grocery stores within minutes, thereby learning the range of prices available in the marketplace). The individual looking to hire an attorney is more likely to accept the pricing offer made by the first attorney who is willing to take on the case.

Because there is no ready marketplace for the services of plaintiffs' attorneys it will be difficult for reformers to develop general rules that balance the need to give plaintiffs access to counsel with the efficiency goals of limiting litigation that is motivated largely by attorneys' fees.

Just Enforce the Laws

One argument that some reformers make is that existing laws would be sufficient if only judges enforced them more consistently. Federal Rule 54(d), for example, provides that "costs other than attorneys' fees shall be allowed as of course" to the prevailing party. That same rule also empowers federal judges to grant an award of attorneys' fees to the prevailing party in the court's discretion. If federal courts did, in fact, award costs and attorneys' fees when parties prevailed it wouldn't be necessary to consider the English rule or the offer of judgment rule as possible reforms.

This argument, however, answers itself. Courts in fact often decline to award costs to the prevailing party and only rarely grant awards of attorneys' fees. If courts are already willing to turn mandatory requirements (i.e., "shall be allowed as of course") into discretionary rules, it is hard to imagine what a legislative solution would do. Judges will always retain the final authority to interpret any legislative solution.

Bad cases make for bad law, as the saying goes, and judges have become accustomed to letting parties get away with weak arguments without consequences. It is easier, as a judge, to let a case slide by than it is to order one party to pay the other's attorneys' fees. The fee award is likely to prompt additional objections and, sometimes, more work for the court, so the easy decision is just to let it go. This is especially true in jurisdictions where judges are elected and may perceive a need to avoid the appearance of handing out harsh results.

Unfortunately, this tendency makes the offer of judgment rule or other fee-shifting rules necessary. Only by putting the power to recover fees back into the hands of the party who pays them can we systematically ensure that blameless parties get reimbursed when entitled.

Conclusion

Some of the alternative reforms I summarized here are worthy of additional thought and effort. There are others not summarized here that may also merit research and study. In time perhaps some of these additional solutions may help to fine tune our litigation system and improve it. By comparing my proposals for capping punitive damages and shifting fees through judgment offers, I am not suggesting that there are no other solutions.

I do believe, however, that my proposals can have the most immediate and significant impact on the overall litigation burden with the least political risk.

9

Common Objections

The need for reform is as urgent today as it ever has been…. It is precisely because the opportunities for progress today are so great that our obstructionist tort system is such great cause for concern. Peter W. Huber, LIABILITY: THE LEGAL REVOLUTION AND ITS CONSEQUENCES (1988).

Among the many opponents of reform, the American Trial Lawyers Association ("ATLA') is one of the most effective. A well-financed organization that generally supports the rights of plaintiffs, the organization boasts more than 56,000 members and a staff of more than 150. The ATLA also has a website for educating the public and getting pro-plaintiff messages to legislators and the media. It has organized dozens of papers on the major issues involving litigation reform under the helpful heading of "Protecting Your Rights". Any serious attempt to reform the civil justice system should expect stiff resistance from the ATLA and other organizations that have a stake in the way the current litigation system works. Summarized below are some of the arguments that the opponents of reform would be expected to make to the Model Statutes I have proposed.

Capping Punitive Damages

Punitive Damages are Small and Rare

One of the chief arguments against any proposal for capping punitive damages is that "punitive damages…aren't awarded as widely "as "reformers" would have people believe"[146] and that when punitive damages are awarded "most punitive damages awards are for less than $40,000."[147] This argument is based upon a

---

146. *See, e.g.,* http://www.atla.org/ConsumerMediaResources/Tier3/press_room/ FACTS/pundam/judges.punitives.bjs.aspx (last visited December 29, 2004). The scare quotes are in the original.

study of state court trials that determined that punitive damages were awarded in only 3.3 percent of the cases won by plaintiffs. Although the website doesn't identify the study by name or date, the quotation from an article in the Wall Street Journal in June 2000 suggests that the study was completed in the late 1990s, several years prior to the studies I cited earlier in this book.

Taking this data at face value, however, it still does not refute the more fundamental problem with punitive damages. In 2002, noneconomic damages from tort cases alone amounted to more than $55 billion. That figure includes both punitive damages and other noneconomic damages like "pain and suffering". Even if punitive damages are only awarded in 3.3 percent of all trials won by plaintiffs that does not change the $55 billion annual cost of noneconomic damages by one penny.

The $40,000 figure for an average punitive damages award also doesn't mean much. In Professor Viscusi's study of state court punitive damages awards under the 1:1 ratio suggested by the reasoning of the Supreme Court's *State Farm* decision, it appeared that 29% of state court punitive damages awards would be invalidated and that these awards amounted to 94% of the total dollar value of all the punitive damages awards made by these state courts.[148] As a result, even if the average dollar value of state court punitive awards were $40,000, a sizeable portion of state court punitive awards would still offend constitutional limits.

In addition, looking at the numbers and amounts of awards actually issued following trial ignores the effect that the existence of uncapped punitive damages can have on the handling and settling of litigation. The statistics on actual punitive awards don't reveal how many cases were filed with claims of punitive damages and how many of those were settled. The statistics also cannot tell us how much money was paid by defendants in settlements reached as a consequence of defendants' fear of fighting punitive damages claims.

Punitive Damages Promote Safety

Another argument that the opponents of reform often make is that punitive damages promote safety or deter wrongdoing. Earlier in Chapter 5 we discussed the studies that reviewed the potential deterrence effects of punitive damages and concluded that they did not, in fact, deter the wrongdoing of defendants or make the products manufactured by them safer.

---

147. *Id.*
148. *See* discussion in Chapter 5, *infra.*

On its website, the ATLA claims, "punitive damage awards guarantee public safety."[149] The ATLA backs up this claim with a list of landmark cases in which individual plaintiffs sued manufacturers of consumer products and recovered massive awards, including awards of punitive damages. In most of the cases cited on the page, the punitive damages were several times greater than the compensatory damages. Elsewhere on its website the ATLA highlights the cases of individuals who suffered horrible injuries but whose punitive damages awards were limited by state laws capping punitive damages. The implication in these stories is that any limitation on punitive damages is a "one size fits all" remedy that unfairly punishes sympathetic victims.

On the key question of whether the presence of uncapped punitive damages promotes safety, neither the ATLA nor any of the anti-reform groups can demonstrate how punitive damages actually make products safer. Nearly all of the big awards cases featured on the ATLA's website date to the 1980s and 1990s. At that time there were relatively few states with any caps on punitive damages. If punitive damages "guarantee" public safety, we should have expected for the injuries complained of in these cases not to have occurred. After all, the injuries took place in an environment in which punitive damages were unlimited. The fact that cases with large, multi-million dollar punitive damages award occurred testifies to the fact that punitive damages did not prevent the injuries in those cases. However sympathetic the individual plaintiffs might be, the millions of dollars in punitive awards they received were a windfall. No one might wish to trade places with these individuals for the money received, but that is not the point. The point is that the presence of uncapped punitive damages did not actually make the public safer.

Incidentally, critics' complaints about "one size fits all" caps to punitive damages has a ring to it and suggests another reason why caps based on the ratio to compensatory damages are better than flat dollar value caps. The flat dollar value caps are arbitrary except where they are linked to a specific kind of case (i.e., a limit of so many dollars in punitive damages in a medical malpractice case, for example). And yet the flat dollar value caps that states have adopted in *Appendix A* are not linked to particular kinds of cases. Adopting a cap on punitive damages of the kind described in the Model Statute in *Appendix B* avoids the "one size fits

---

149. http://www.atla.org/ConsumerMediaResources/Tier3/press_room/FACTS/ pundam/punitive%20damages%20cases%20that%20made%20a%20 difference.aspx.

all" argument and allows an injured plaintiff to recover punitive damages that are proportionate to its actual damages.

Punitive Damages Award the Efforts of Plaintiffs

One argument that you won't find on the ATLA's website although it is often raised in the academic literature is that plaintiffs need to have the availability of uncapped punitive damages in order to "reward" them for bringing cases. The rationale is that many injured victims do not actually pursue their cases in court. They either conclude that litigation is "not worth it" or is too time consuming or for some other reason determine that they don't want to press their cases. Thus, the argument goes, in every situation in which a deserving potential plaintiff drops its case the defendant enjoys a windfall, measured by the damages it did not have to pay and the expenses it did not have to incur. Some academics have described this theoretical windfall as an "under-deterrence gap" because, to the extent that it exists, it undermines the supposed deterrent effect of punitive damages. The under-deterrence gap, the argument goes, allows defendants to sustain repeated claims for compensatory damages and still come out ahead. To avoid this windfall effect, the plaintiffs who do pursue their claims should be able to collect substantial punitive damages to consume the defendant's windfall from the cases that other plaintiffs chose not to pursue.

For obvious reasons this is an argument that public policy groups will rarely make in debates over legislative reforms and it is one that is easily debunked as well. First, even if potential defendants enjoy a windfall when potential plaintiffs drop their cases, that is no different from the windfall that actual plaintiffs enjoy when they settle questionable cases against actual defendants because the high cost of defense makes settlement the means of greatest cost avoidance. Also, assuming that society is harmed by an under-deterrence gap, how does it benefit society for plaintiffs to recover the benefit? By definition, a plaintiff that receives all of its compensatory damages has been made whole. Punitive damages (even at the ratio of 1:1) are still a windfall to the plaintiff. Giving one particular plaintiff the economic benefit of the windfall enjoyed by the defendant in other cases neither does justice for that plaintiff or for society.

Once you determine that punitive damages play no role in promoting safety or in deterring wrongdoing, it is hard to justify punitive damages at all.

Shifting Attorneys Fees

Because reforms based upon fee-shifting and offers of judgment are rather rare and have not received much attention in either the popular or the scholarly media, there are no pat answers to the offer of judgment proposal made in *Appendix C.* I have tried, however, to marshal the arguments that the opponents of reform are mostly likely to make.

Shifting Fees Will Promote Excessive Defense Costs

One possible argument is that if a defendant is able to shift its costs to the plaintiff by making an offer of judgment that the plaintiff declines, defendants will have an incentive to hire the most expensive attorneys and generally to overspend on the defense.

In truth, corporate defendants already spend more on defense than do plaintiffs. This is more a function of the interests that corporate defendants serve, however, than a desire on the part of corporate decision-makers to buy the most expensive lawyers possible. A corporate defendant managing a lawsuit faces a number of prerogatives, including the need to show results for corporate managers and the need to avoid a litigation loss that will not only cost money but damage the company's reputation. As a result, the way in which defense lawyers manage cases is very different than for plaintiffs' lawyers.

As we discussed in Chapter 2, the litigation process allows defendants the opportunity to dismiss the case before trial at the preliminary motions stage and at the summary judgment stage. In the preliminary motions stage, the defendant must prove that even if all of the plaintiff's claims are true, the law still does not allow the plaintiff to recover. At the summary judgment stage, the defendant must prove that even if all of the evidence is interpreted in the light most favorable to the plaintiff, it still will not have enough evidence to persuade a reasonable jury that it should recover. Managing a case to prevail at one of these two stages requires a careful attention to detail and a careful study of the legal precedents. For example, in taking depositions in the discovery process skillful defense lawyers will already know what the key facts will be (based upon prior court cases) that will make the case appropriate for dismissal. Defense lawyers will make certain to pull those particular facts out of the witness when taking a deposition.

Although some plaintiffs' lawyers can be quite skillful, as a generality plaintiffs' lawyers usually do not pay as much attention as defense lawyers to prior cases at the outset of litigation. Plaintiffs' lawyers tend to focus more on the equities of the case and whether the plaintiff will appear sympathetic. Plaintiffs' lawyers are also more likely to focus on circumstances that look like "bad facts" to the defendant, like an internal memo or document that suggests that the defendant knew it was doing something wrong. Even if these "bad facts" have no legal impact (in a technical sense) plaintiffs' lawyers tend to focus on them as much for their emotional appeal as anything else. This kind of focus, of course, while it may require skill does not require the painstaking attention and advance planning that defense work requires. As a result, when measured purely by billable hours defense work tends to be more expensive.

The economics of defense law practice also tends to make defense lawyers more expensive. Plaintiffs' lawyers have numerous clients, generally one for every case. It is fairly rare for a plaintiffs' lawyer to have the same client pursuing more than one case at a time. Defense lawyers, on the other hand, rely upon relationships with companies and entrepreneurs to generate work. Publicly traded companies with in-house attorneys may have relationships with litigators at outside law firms whom they supply with a continuing supply of work. Relying on a smaller group of clients for more of their workload, defense lawyers perceive little room for error. They worry that if they lose a case their client might move other cases to a different lawyer or firm. As a result, defense lawyers have very strong incentives to turn out high quality work and will often invest more time and effort in defeating a case than will a plaintiffs' lawyer in prosecuting that case.

Taking these considerations into account, it is not surprising that, even without a fee-shifting rule, defendants often spend more on attorneys than do plaintiffs. The question becomes whether adopting a fee-shifting rule would give defendants more of an incentive than they already have to over-defend their cases. On balance that is not very likely.

First, because I have not proposed a pure English rule but rather a fee-shifting scheme that depends upon an offer of judgment, the defendant can never be certain that he will win back his attorneys' fees. He could guess wrong and the plaintiff who declines his judgment offer might well prevail with a greater-than-anticipated recovery. In that event the defendant would bear his own fees and pay the recovery to the plaintiff.

Even if the defendant were thoroughly convinced that the plaintiff's recovery would fall short of the defendant's offer of judgment, a defendant that over-spent on defense would still have to pay its legal fees as they were incurred. Prevailing on the case and winning a right to recover attorneys' fees might take months or even years. In addition, even if the defendant prevailed there could be no guarantee that it would be able to collect its attorneys' fees from the unhappy plaintiff. If the plaintiff lacked the assets to satisfy the attorneys' fee award, the defendant might have a moral victory, but no money to show for it.

On balance, it is hard to see how the fee-shifting proposal would give additional incentives to defendants to inflate their attorneys' fees.

Shifting Fees Will Deny Access to the Poor

Perhaps the most potent argument that reform opponents will have to a fee-shifting reform is that this will prevent the poor from having access to the courts. Of course, this "lack of access" argument is not literal. Plaintiffs will still be able to sue regardless of their means. What the opponents will argue is that the fear of having to reimburse the defendant's attorneys' fees will chill plaintiffs into dropping their claims or settling them for too low of an amount.

What is ironic about this argument is that fears attached to the potential for liability are much more of a problem for middle and upper-middle class persons than they are for the truly poor. An individual with no net worth who is charged with a substantial liability can often avoid that liability through a personal bankruptcy. Having no net worth to begin with, the truly poor individual loses no assets through the bankruptcy and may actually qualify for more government benefits as a bankrupt than before. The middle or upper-middle class person with significant retirement savings, however, properly fears losing those savings in litigation. A personal bankruptcy of a person with significant savings could wipe out those savings, generating greater loss for the individual than in the case of the individual with no net worth.

Even so, would it defeat the equity goals of the justice system if plaintiffs feared for their financial security in pursuing litigation against well-heeled corporate defendants? If so, would this necessarily be unfair?

Not all defendants, of course, are corporations. When an individual gets sued that individual often has little option other than to settle at the plaintiff's mercy. As we've discussed, the cost of contesting a civil case can quickly mount into the tens of thousands, a level that most ordinary people would find insurmountable. Having no ability to recover attorneys' fees if they win, many individual defendants find it better to pay the plaintiffs' demand, rather than risk their net worth on the attorneys' fees required to resist.

On the contrary, it is the current system that gives plaintiffs a free shot at defendants. Only the plaintiff can determine whether it is truly worth the risk to pursue a claim. If the defendant is willing to offer the plaintiff a judgment, only the plaintiff can judge whether it is worth the risk to pursue the claim rather than accepting the settlement offer. The current system effectively patronizes plaintiffs by shielding them from the responsibility of their own choices. Having no responsibility, and bearing no risk, the current system encourages plaintiffs to act irresponsibly, forcing defendants to spend their money defending cases that aren't worth the cost.

If a fee-shifting proposal discourages some plaintiffs from pursuing their claims and encourages other plaintiffs to settle for less than they hoped to get at trial, that will be better than the status quo. The offer of judgment proposal increases the menu of choices available to both parties in litigation. In the current system, the defendant has no choice but to defend itself or else plead with the plaintiff to accept its settlement offers. By giving the defendant the choice of making a settlement offer that comes with fee-shifting, reformers improve the ability of the parties to place values on their choices. That should encourage the swifter resolution of cases and that will reduce the overall burden of litigation.

Shifting Fees Will Only Benefit Big Companies

A consistent theme in the rhetoric of the ATLA and some of the other organizations that oppose civil justice reform is that reform only benefits "big corporations" and "the rich". Somehow, they suggest, reforming the litigation process will fleece average Americans and enrich wealthy corporations.

This kind of rhetoric is well-worn, so much so that it has lost much of the impact it used to have, and yet the ATLA and some of the other opponents of reform continue to use these kind of class warfare arguments. The ATLA even uses seemingly independent websites, like the "People Over Profits" Organization, to couch its anti-reform arguments in terms that sound proletarian.[150]

Using class warfare as a means of opposing litigation reform is a bit of a stretch for the trial lawyer lobby. As Walter Olson points out in The Rule of Lawyers, many of the country's leading trial lawyers are extremely wealthy.[151] The fees awarded to plaintiffs' attorneys in large class action cases can easily amount to thousands of dollars per hour worked. Trial lawyers recognize that their incomes rely upon the continued willingness of legislators to avoid changing the procedural rules that make their kind of lucrative litigation possible. As a result, trial

---

150. *See* http://www.peopleoverprofits.org. The ATLA's website contains links to the People Over Profits organization. The People Over Profits website's registered address in the WHOIS database is the same as the ATLA's Washington, D.C. headquarters. (Last visited December 29, 2004).
151. *See generally*, Olson, THE RULE OF LAWYERS, *supra* n77.

lawyers individually make up some of the largest contributors to political campaigns and the ATLA routinely ranks among the top five political contributors in the country[152].

While the offer of judgment rule will doubtless help defendants bring plaintiffs to consider offers of settlement and should encourage more plaintiffs to settle litigation at earlier stages, to say that it would benefit "big corporations" is like saying that the U.S. national defense benefits big corporations because they have more to lose. The point of reform is not to benefit any one group of litigants over another, but rather to restore balance into the system. The offer of judgment rule is party-neutral; it can be used by defendants on the plaintiff's claims and by the plaintiff on the defendant's counterclaims. If it works to benefit corporations (whether big or small) that is only because they are more likely to be sued than individuals who lack the financial resources of corporations.

Even if this argument was more than an appeal to prejudice, what is wrong with corporations? Corporations that increase their profits either spend those profits, thereby spurring the economy or they distribute their profits in dividends to their shareholders. Nearly 50% of all Americans own stock in corporations, either directly as stockholders or indirectly through mutual funds and retirement plans.[153] Even Americans who have no ownership interest in the stock market rely on corporations for the products they buy and for their jobs.

This is an age-old argument but one that bears repeating when the opponents of reform try to play the class warfare card in this debate. Expensive litigation doesn't benefit the poor and it doesn't benefit the middle class. It only benefits the plaintiffs' lawyers who make their living generating legal fees. Expensive litigation acts like a tax on all Americans, with its brunt felt the most by the poor and the middle class. Reforming the litigation system and lessening the burdens of litigation will benefit everyone, especially those who have the least.

The Problem of the Perfect Plaintiff

Perhaps the most powerful argument that can be summoned against a fee-shifting offer of judgment rule is that it carries with it the potential to deprive some plaintiffs of a full recovery for their injuries. This argument suggests that a blameless plaintiff, who has unquestionable injuries and an unquestionable right of recov-

---

152. Jim Copland, *Primary Pass*, National Review Online (January 26, 2004), *available at* http://www.nationalreview.com/comment/ copland200401260836.asp

153. Congressional Joint Economic Committee Study, *The Roots of Broadened Stock Ownership* (2000) *available at* http://www.house.gov/jec/tax/stock/stock.htm.

ery for 100% of its injuries, might be intimidated by an offer of judgment into settling for less than 100%. Even having faith in its case, the plaintiff might fear the risk of having to pay the defendant's attorneys' fees and might therefore accept less than complete justice to avoid that risk. It's important to understand why this argument should not derail enthusiasm for an offer of judgment rule.

At the outset, this argument is, at least partially, a victim of its own premise. How often is it that you find a plaintiff with unquestionable injuries and an unquestionable right of recovery? No statistical evidence can be possible but experience suggests that this is a rarity. Nearly any case that is contested is so because at least one party believes the outcome is in doubt. As a result, to assume a "perfect" plaintiff with an unquestionable right of recovery is to assume a situation that is exceedingly rare.

Even if we assume such a perfect plaintiff, the offer of judgment rule's economic incentives work to the benefit of that plaintiff. If the defendant makes an offer of judgment that is significantly less than the plaintiff's unquestionable right of recovery the plaintiff has every right to push forward with litigation and the defendant receives no benefit from its parsimonious offer. The greater the difference between the offer of judgment and the plaintiff's true damages, the less urgency the plaintiff will perceive towards settlement. The real problem, opponents may suggest, is when the defendant/offeror gets close to the plaintiff's ideal outcome (say, 90%) but still less than 100% of the plaintiff's real entitlement.

How unfair would this be? If you were the plaintiff, you might feel unfairly treated by settling for less than 100% of your damages. On the other hand, the choice to settle would be yours and, by settling, you would recover the offered amount immediately, without the delay or uncertainty of litigation. You would retain the power to choose settlement or litigation but you would be accountable for that choice.

Would the perfect plaintiff's loss of some percentage of the perfect recovery be that unfair? Fairness is a matter of perspective. Legislators should compare what might feel unfair to some individual plaintiffs to the unfairness felt by millions of defendants every year that must pay 100% of their attorneys' fees for the privilege of being vindicated.

Imagine the inverse of the "perfect plaintiff": the "unworthy plaintiff". This hypothetical plaintiff has no real injuries and absolutely no reasonable claim against the defendant. Under the current system, the defendant pays 100% of its attorneys' fees for the right to pay the plaintiff nothing. That's unfair. Under a fee-shifting offer of judgment rule a defendant sued by a perfectly unworthy plaintiff will likely offer a small amount in order to shift the risk of attorneys' fees onto the unworthy plaintiff. Is *this* fair for the defendant? Not entirely.

The defendant will *still* spend a small amount on attorneys' fees, if on nothing more than reading the complaint and preparing the offer of judgment. The defendant will *still* pay the amount of the offered judgment (assuming that it is accepted). If so, the outcome will *still* be a net negative for the defendant (although a less negative outcome than under the current system). If the perfectly unworthy plaintiff is foolish enough to persist despite an offered judgment, the defendant will *still* have to pay its attorneys fees throughout the course of the litigation until, perhaps a year or more later, the defendant recovers a fee award against the unworthy plaintiff. Even then, however, the defendant will *still* need to pay attorneys to enforce the fee award, a process that could take even more months. Of course even the defendant who recovers a fee award can only enforce it to the extent that the plaintiff has assets to satisfy it. If the plaintiff lacks the funds to pay the fee award, the defendant will *never* receive what it is fairly due.

Viewed from a larger perspective—the perspective that legislators ought to adopt—any unfairness suffered by a few, rare "perfect plaintiffs" is more than offset by that suffered by defendants at the hands of perfectly "unworthy plaintiffs". The fee-shifting offer of judgment rule minimizes the unfairness and economic waste present in the current system but cannot reduce the unfairness and waste to zero. The outcome, in a system that has been rebalanced through reform, is not perfect but is far more fairly balanced than the status quo.

10

Political Progress on Reform

Sometimes, like a staggering alcoholic, a state has to hit rock bottom before a majority of legislators become convinced that changes must occur. Charlie Ross, Winning the Tort War in Mississippi: Keys for Success in Other States (2004).

The 2004 presidential election sparked some discussion over the need to reform the civil justice system and that discussion brings some hope to those who have been advocating reform for so long. It was noteworthy that even the democratic nominee for vice-president, Senator John Edwards from North Carolina, who is a plaintiffs' attorney, admitted there were "too many lawsuits" and that reform was needed to reduce the number of lawsuits. To some degree, then, there is bipartisan agreement that some kind of change is needed.

Efforts in the States

The bulk of the work on litigation reform must necessarily be done in the states because state courts handle more than ninety percent of all the civil litigation in the country. This makes an organized national campaign for reform difficult because it needs to account for the individualized needs of each state and already existing variations in state laws.

Reform in Ohio

In December 2004 the Ohio General Assembly passed measures to restrict litigation in Ohio courts.[154] The Ohio legislation, Senate Bill 80, contained a laundry

---

154. Ohio Senate Bill 80, 125th General Assembly of Ohio, *available at* http://www. legislature.state.oh.us/bills.cfm?ID=125_SB_80.

list of reforms, including limitations on pain and suffering damages in cases that were not "catastrophic" to $500,000, a "statute of repose" that limits the ability to bring product liability suits beyond 10 years after the purchase of an allegedly defective product, and the abolition of the collateral source rule, allowing defendants to offset their liability by introducing evidence that a plaintiff had already been compensated for its losses through another source. Although Ohio Governor Bob Taft had not yet signed the law by the time this book went to print, he had praised the law and indicated his intention of signing it, saying, "A fair and effective civil justice system is an essential part of promoting and sustaining an attractive business climate in Ohio."[155]

Commentators in Ohio praised the bill, claiming that by limiting litigation the bill would encourage businesses to stay in Ohio and even to move to Ohio from other states:

> "Businesses believe the reform could lessen the climate of uncertainty in which they've operated, unsure when that "killer" lawsuit would come. The stability and predictability they think it will bring could aid Ohio's economy in the long run, encouraging businesses to stay or move here. If so—and especially if the courts uphold the reform's constitutionality—that would be a long-term win for Ohio."[156]

Perhaps most importantly, Ohio's S.B. 80 was the first legislative attempt to cap punitive damages based upon a ratio of compensatory damages after the Supreme Court's guidance in the *State Farm* case. In the bill's legislative findings, the legislature cited much of the economic data discussed earlier in this book, including the rising cost of litigation nationwide, the effect of the litigation tax, and the general inefficiency of litigation as a method of compensating individuals for their injuries.[157] S.B. 80 also expressly cited the *State Farm* case and indicated that its legislative approach was intended to tie punitive damages to a ratio of two times compensatory damages in the manner proposed by the Supreme Court in that case.[158]

---

155. *Ohio Sets New Lawsuit Limits*, Cincinnati Enquirer (December 10, 2004) *available at* http://news.enquirer.com/apps/pbcs.dll/article?AID=/20041210/BIZ01/ 412100347/1002.

156. Editorial, *Tort Reform Could Be Winner For Ohio*, Cincinnati Enquirer (December 13, 2004), *available at* http://news.enquirer.com/apps/pbcs.dll/article?AID=/ 20041213/EDIT01/412130304/1020.

157. Ohio S.B. 80, *supra* n154 at Section 3.

Reform in California

Voters in California, a state that many defense lawyers had held up as an example of the worst failings of the civil justice system, took it upon themselves in 2004 to modify one of the strangest and most pro-plaintiff statutes ever adopted in the United States, California's Unfair Competition Law 17200 ("UCL 17200").

UCL 17200 was amended by the California legislature in 1963 to include some of the provisions that proved to be problematic by the 1990s. The purpose of the statute was to empower private individuals, and private lawyers of course, to enforce any instance of "unfair competition" they found in a private suit against the perpetrator. Several features of the law made it especially prone to abuse. First, through its language, UCL 17200 effectively incorporated by reference every other state and federal law, making virtually any violation of any law a violation of UCL 17200. In essence, any action that violated any law anywhere could be made into a private right of action under UCL 17200.

Next, the statute turned the traditional legal concept of "standing" on its head. The rule of standing, which is a constitutional principle in federal courts, is taken from the express language in Article III of the Constitution requiring that only a party with a direct interest in a matter can initiate a lawsuit on that matter. For example, if I observe that you are the victim of a tort no matter how much I might sympathize with your plight I cannot sue the tortfeasor in your place. Only you would have "standing" to vindicate your own rights in a lawsuit. UCL 17200, on the other hand, empowered any private attorney in California to file a lawsuit to stop any violation of law regardless of whether the attorney had a client who was actually harmed by that violation. In essence, the law gave *carte blanche* to every plaintiffs' lawyer in California to sue anyone that ever violated any law.

Not surprisingly, when laws give incentives to attorneys to file lots of lawsuits, they do. UCL 17200 quickly became one of the most abused statutes in the country as attorneys quickly organized virtual shake-down operations, filing lawsuits against any business they could find that had any kind of potentially illegal practice. Because the suing attorneys had no real client in interest, they could effectively leverage the law to require defendants to pay their attorneys fees as part of a settlement.

Examples of plaintiffs' attorneys abusing the law proliferated. One attorney filed suit under UCL 17200 against nearly two hundred travel agents who had

---

158. *Id.* S.B. 80 also further limits awards of punitive damages against certain kinds of small businesses to an amount not exceeding the lesser of twice compensatory damages or $350,000.

websites that failed to include a copy of California's Seller of Travel code. Another case was filed against Black & Decker and other hardware stores that sold a lock advertised as "Made in the U.S.A." Although the lock was assembled entirely in the United States and composed primarily of parts made in the United States, the lock allegedly included six screws manufactured in Taiwan. A group of homebuilders were sued under UCL 17200 because their advertisements used the abbreviation "APR" instead of the term "Annual Percentage Rate" as specified in federal law governing the publication of interest rates. (Because UCL 17200 incorporates by reference both California state and federal laws, it effectively took a federal law and authorized its enforcement in a way never intended by Congress). One UCL 17200 case was filed against a health club over the language in its three-day-right-of-cancellation clause. The language, which was required by a California statute, failed to note that Sundays and holidays were excluded in the calculation of the three days.[159]

As UCL 17200 became the subject of ridicule, it began to attract the attention of judges. In one case an attorney used his mother to create a corporation, Stop Youth Addiction, Inc., which in turn sued several thousand convenience stores for violating a provision of California law that prohibited the sale of cigarettes to minors. Although the corporation had no assets, no employees and no revenues (except for the proceeds of its lawsuits) the California Supreme Court allowed the corporation's lawsuit to proceed. The attorney's mother, who was the sole stockholder of the corporation, admitted that the corporation's only function was to file lawsuits and that her attorney's only income was "from people who lost their cases, he gets attorney fees."[160]

Although the California Supreme Court allowed the lawsuit to continue, in dissent, Justice Janice Rogers Brown decried the majority's willingness to interpret the law to permit parties with no real interest in the matter to litigate cases on behalf of the public. She reasoned that, although political concerns and prosecutorial discretion might guide the decisions of public prosecutors in deciding how to prosecute in criminal cases, no similar concerns restrained the "private attorneys general" permitted by UCL 17200. By allowing private attorneys to manufacture lawsuits, she wrote, "the majority chooses to speed us along the path to perdition, genially opting for the worst of all possible legal worlds: abuse of process…extortionate nuisance lawsuits, confusion and duplication of litigation

---

159. Examples cited on a website sponsoring Proposition 64,
    http://www.stopshakedownlawsuits.com/facts_examples.html.
160. *Stop Youth Addiction, Inc. v. Lucky Stores, Inc.*, 17 Cal. 4th 553 at 586 (1998) (Brown, J. dissenting).

resources and uncertain finality."[161] She concluded that the statute had become "a standardless, limitless, attorney fees machine."[162]

Fearing that the legislature would be unable to muster the political will to modify the statute, reformers turned to California's unique referendum procedure to take reform to the voters. The effort, which became known as Proposition 64, remedied only the worst aspect of UCL 17200, the provision that allows anyone to sue under the law, regardless of their lack of standing.[163] The measure, which was approved by California voters on November 2, 2004, amended the standing provisions of UCL 17200 so that actions under the law could only be brought by a person "who has suffered injury in fact and has lost money or property as a result of such unfair competition."

While UCL 17200 still remains an awful law because of the way it incorporates by reference almost any other alleged legal violation, it is less awful under the reform brought by Proposition 64. What was especially interesting about the reform effort, however, was the fact that it was an initiative taken directly to the voters. Proponents spoke directly to voters about the problem of frivolous litigation and explained the economic impact of litigation and how that impact ultimately affected consumers as well as businesses. In an election that represented the greatest turnout in American political history[164] the voters of California by a margin of 59% approved Proposition 64, proving that voters can be persuaded of the merits of reforming the litigation system.[165] The support was bipartisan as California voters in the same election supported the Democratic nominee for President by a substantial margin.

Reform in Mississippi

Mississippi was once known for its pro-plaintiff environment and had been derided by some reform groups as being a "judicial hellhole" and representing the "jackpot justice capital of America."[166] Perhaps this growing reputation and the burden it was imposing on the state was the impetus for a reform effort in Missis-

---

161. *Id.* (citations omitted).
162. *Id.* at 598.
163. Proposition 64, *available at* http://caag.state.ca.us/initiatives/pdf/sa2003rf0051.pdf#search='proposition%2064'.
164. http://www.cnn.com/ELECTION/2004/pages/results/.
165. *Businesses Hail Prop. 64 Victory*, Sacramento Bee (Nov. 4, 2004) *available at* http://www.sacbee.com/content/news/courts_legal/story/11314760p-12229602c.html.
166. American Tort Reform Association, *Bringing Justice to Judicial Hellholes* (2003).

sippi that took several years but culminated in a series of litigation reform bills in 2004.[167]

In 2004 the Mississippi legislature, working through a special session called by Governor Haley Barbour for the purpose of considering litigation reform, passed a comprehensive measure that enacted a number of changes.[168] The new law, which took effect September 1, 2004, limits forum-shopping, caps noneconomic damages at $1 million (except in certain medical cases), limits punitive damages and abolishes the traditional rule of joint and several liability.

Charlie Ross, the chair of the Mississippi Senate Judiciary Committee and one of the architects of the 2004 litigation reform bill, credited a number of factors for the passage of the legislation. The reform took several years and several efforts, during which the supporters of reform were able to work through their arguments and educate legislators on the issues. After developing a consensus, the groups supporting reform worked to craft a message that took the complicated procedures involved in litigation and crafted them in common sense terms that made sense to voters. The reformers made sure to limit their legislative package to a series of reforms that could be justified on the merits, even though that sometimes meant leaving behind a measure that might have been important to one or another interest group. The effort, Senator Ross noted, also had the support of the state's governor, who was instrumental in using his bully pulpit to communicate the need for reform through the media.[169]

Reform in Texas

Reform efforts in Mississippi took their cue, at least in part, from the success of reform efforts in Texas in 2003. With a reputation that was similar to Mississippi's for being a "playground for pillaging trial lawyers"[170] the Texas legislature passed a comprehensive litigation reform package[171] that included:

---

167. Charlie Ross, *Winning the Tort War in Mississippi: Keys for Success in Other States*, *available at* http://www.atra.org.

168. H.B. 13, 2004 Leg., 1st Ex. Sess. (Miss. 2004) *available at* http://billstatus.ls.state.ms.us/documents/20041E/html/HB/0001-0099/HB0013SG.htm.

169. *See generally*, Ross, *supra* n167.

170. Hugh Rice Kelly, *2003 Reform Legislation in Texas: "Ten Gallon Tort Reform"* (2004) available at http://www.tortreform.com.

171. Texas H.B. 78 *supra* n128.

- guaranteed immediate appeal of class certification decisions;

- a fee-shifting offer of judgment rule;

- procedural rules intended to prevent plaintiffs from "shopping" cases in search of sympathetic judges in certain districts;

- elimination of joint and several liability among joint tortfeasors and adoption of a rule of "proportionate responsibility";

- a 15-year statute of repose for product liability claims;

- an "innocent retailer" defense for product liability claims;

- limitations on the size of appeal bonds (limited to the lesser of 50% of the defendant's net worth or $25 million); and

- caps on noneconomic damages and other reforms.

Reform Efforts in Congress

In June 2004, Congressman Lamar Smith (R-TX) introduced H.R. 4571 entitled the Lawsuit Abuse Reduction Act (hereinafter, "LARA").[172] The LARA was amended in the House before it was passed in September 2004 by a vote of 229-174. The version of the bill that passed the House could have had a significant effect on litigation in federal and state courts.[173] In essence, the LARA would have made sanctions for filing frivolous lawsuits or motions under Federal Rule 11 mandatory rather than at the discretion of the judge. Such sanctions were mandatory when Rule 11 was originally adopted in 1983 but were made discretionary in 1993.

In addition, the LARA added two additional provisions to Rule 11 that could have had even more far-reaching effects. First, in the version of the bill passed by the House, an attorney who was sanctioned for violating Rule 11 three times in his career would be suspended from practicing in federal courts for at least one year, with the court having the discretion to suspend the attorney for an even longer term. In addition, the bill purported to empower parties in state court litigation to move the court to make a determination whether the state court action

---

172. Lawsuit Abuse Reduction Act, H.R. 4571, 108th Cong., 2nd Sess. (June 15, 2004) *available at* http://thomas.loc.gov/cgi-bin/query/D?c108:1:./temp/~c108u3rn0V...
173. Marcia Coyle, National Law Journal (September 27, 2004).

affected interstate commerce. If the state court found that the action affected interstate commerce, the bill provided that Rule 11 (prohibiting parties from pursuing legally frivolous claims) would apply in the state court proceeding.

Coming just a few months before the 2004 general election, the issue divided legislators on partisan lines and the measure did not receive any action in the Senate. The LARA would have made a significant difference if it had become law. By making sanctions under Rule 11 mandatory, the measure would have lowered the bar for the imposition of sanctions. The "three strikes and you're out" rule would have significantly increased the seriousness of any sanction under Rule 11, putting individual lawyers in fear for their livelihoods for pursuing frivolous actions. By allowing state courts to adopt Rule 11 on a case by case basis upon the motion of a party, the bill would have federalized much of the law of frivolous litigation and would have empowered state judges to punish frivolous tactics in ways not otherwise permitted under state laws. Although this federalization of the law undoubtedly would have been challenged on constitutional grounds, it was a measure of the determination of legislators to deter excessive litigation that such a far-ranging measure went as far as it did in an election year.

The 108th Congress also considered possible changes in federal class action law through the Class Action Fairness Act.[174] Although the reforms proposed in this bill would have modified some of the procedural rules governing class actions, most of the reforms were fairly technical and left the bulk of existing class action law unchanged.

Nevertheless, even the potential for changing the rules in a way that would limit speculative lawsuits brought out the opponents of reform in force. The Democratic members of the Senate Judiciary Committee which heard the bill agreed that "class action litigation has genuine problems that should be addressed" but claimed that the Class Action Fairness Act would have undercut the principles of federalism by requiring substantially all class actions in federal, rather than state, courts.[175]

The brunt of the opposition focused on an attempt to characterize the procedural changes, which would have undoubtedly had the effect of forcing many class actions from state court into federal court, as somehow being anti-plaintiff. The opponents claimed that, by requiring more of the cases to be in federal court, "consumers, victims and the environment" would have been hurt because federal

---

174. Class Action Fairness Act of 2003, S.B. 274 (108th Cong. 1st Sess.). *See also* discussion in Chapter 8.
175. Senate Report 108-123, *supra* n40 at 75.

courts are "more expensive…to litigate cases…and force plaintiffs to travel long distances to attend proceedings."[176]

While federal courts do have more formal requirements and can impose higher filing fees, it would be inaccurate to suggest that poor, huddled masses of plaintiffs will be left at the courthouse doors without the funds to take their cases inside. The attorneys who today organize class actions in state courts are well heeled and often quite wealthy. The procedural formalities of federal court may frustrate their aims by hampering weak cases, but they will not pose an insurmountable hurdle to truly meritorious causes. In light of the billions of dollars wasted on excessive litigation, the marginal expense of federal versus state litigation seems inconsequential.

In an interesting twist of the argument, the opponents characterized the reformers' refusal to include amendments specifically focused on firearm and tobacco litigation as evidence that the reformers wanted to protect these industries by maintaining class action rules that were neutral. Hope remains, however, as many of the supporters of the 2003 Class Action Fairness Act have indicated that they will continue to support it and similar measures.[177]

Talking Sensibly About Law and Economics

The examples of Ohio, California, Mississippi and Texas and President Bush's endorsement of litigation reform in the 2004 campaign make the coming years a hopeful time for reforming the American litigation system. The need for reform is bipartisan even though some interest groups will be opposed. The difficulty for reformers will be maintaining media attention and momentum on the issue of reform as more pressing issues and stories come to the fore. To do that, reformers need to express the need for reform and their proposals in terms that voters find appealing and that resonate with principles of common sense.

Personalizing the problem of runaway litigation means taking the macroeconomic concepts of waste and inefficiency and translating them into terms that affect voters personally. Studies that describe the $200+ billion in annual excess litigation costs as amounting to more than $800 per person or more than $3,200 every year for a family of four are a start. Voters can also make value choices on the issue when the cost of excess litigation amounts to a 10% tax on the wages of an average family.

---

176. *Id.* at 79.
177. *See, e.g.*, http://www.uschamber.com/government/issues/reform/classaction.htm.

When asked the question in terms of choices between competing values, voters choose to place limitations on litigation. In a recent survey, 54% of Americans favored legislation to limit the cost of malpractice liability and 72% favored legislation that guaranteed the full payment of lost wages and medical expenses (i.e. economic damages) but that placed reasonable limits on awards for "pain and suffering" (i.e., noneconomic damages).[178]

Value choices are also clear when reformers compare the billions wasted on litigation to other budgetary items at the federal level. The $286 billion wasted on litigation inefficiency in 2003 was more than the total amount paid in corporate income tax by every corporation in America.

But more than numbers and statistics, personalizing the debate over litigation reform requires asking some tough questions. Although there are more than 6 million civil lawsuits filed every year, few individuals have ever been a plaintiff in a lawsuit. Most individuals are strangers to the courtroom and have never tried their hands at litigation. Ask voters whether they would prefer to have a theoretical right to sue under the rules that exist today or whether they would prefer to have the $1,000 or more that they will pay for litigation in 2005 and every year thereafter. Voters who answer that question will almost always opt for reform. The immediate impact of reducing excessive litigation, when it can be quantified for the individual voter, will certainly seem more important that the prospect of someday being involved in a lawsuit.

This is not mere sophistry but an exercise in facilitating voter choice. Isn't it more reasonable for the average voter to prefer repealing the litigation tax, realizing an immediate savings, than to prefer the current litigation system? If few voters will ever avail themselves of the courts in a civil suit, shouldn't voters rationally prefer the immediate impact of cash savings to the theoretical possibility that their prospects in a future lawsuit might be diminished?

The success of reforms in Ohio, California, Mississippi and Texas also demonstrate the need for business interests to band together on the kinds of reform that are systematic, rather than self-interested. Too often in the past reforms have been limited to particular industries or to particular kinds of litigation. For example, in the mid-1990s the Congress reformed securities litigation involving publicly traded companies. Previous reform efforts in the states have targeted medical malpractice suits, asbestos litigation, litigation over firearms manufacturers, litigation involving mold in home construction and other narrow topics. While each of these types of lawsuits may greatly concern the industries involved, it is diffi-

---

178. Common Good, *Polling Data Fact Sheet, supra* n16.

cult to present them to voters as anything other than an attempt by industry to protect itself. By staging the battle around the anecdotes that industry-specific reforms make easy, reformers have too often lost the public relations war when anti-reform interest groups have claimed that the proponents are doing nothing more than protecting themselves from liability.

Reform makes the most sense for voters when it is reform for its own sake and not reform built around a particular constituency. While it may be difficult to build broader coalitions around the concept of economic inefficiency, doing so not only results in better reform legislation but also shifts the focus from the avoidance of liability to the improvement of the process. On this ground the opponents of reform have much less leverage.

Developing business coalitions for litigation reform is also difficult because of the short-term goals that too-often drive business. Public companies need to publish their earnings results every three months and often make decisions based upon the impact on quarterly profits. Private companies must maintain profitability to pay their employees and their suppliers. It is difficult to get business owners and executives to spend money on issues that require a long-term view.

Particularizing the need for reform becomes the solution to this problem as well. Ask a business owner or an executive how much its company would spend defending itself against a frivolous lawsuit. The answer is generally not less than $50,000 and could reach into the hundreds of thousands of dollars. Under the current system, businesses have almost no defense against frivolous lawsuits. The potential for meritless litigation is a time bomb that is ticking in the treasury of every American business. To paraphrase Rick in *Casablanca*, "maybe not tomorrow but someday" that bomb will go off and the business will be forced to spend tens of thousands every month for many months to defend itself against that lawsuit. How much would the executive be willing to pay out of earnings today to contribute to an effort that might prevent that time bomb from exploding?

Although reformers can do better at particularizing and personalizing the economic impacts of wasteful litigation, the story of reform cannot be told entirely through anecdotes. Isolated stories are the ammunition that the opponents of reform will use most effectively. It is simply all too easy to find one or more examples of sympathetic individuals who have been injured in a products liability case or in a medical malpractice case and who have come to represent the opponents' response to reform. The injured individual will testify before the legislative committee, or speak at a press conference while the legislature is in session, in tearful and halting terms over their injuries, how their lives have changed and how, were it not for the gallant efforts of their attorney who sued to recover their damages, they would be impoverished and so on.

Handling these kinds of pro-plaintiff stories is difficult. The injured individuals appear sympathetic because they are. Reform opponents will be careful only to trot out witnesses like this who have been carefully vetted to make sure that they did not contribute to their injuries and were truly undeserving of the misery that befell them. While these witnesses tell stories that are heartbreaking and do in fact represent their personal experiences, they do not tell the entire story that is at the heart of the need for litigation reform. It is much harder to put a face on the frivolous lawsuits, the lawyer-driven settlements and the shakedown class actions than on a handful of accident victims.

Responding to stories that are aimed at arousing voter sympathies requires a careful and systematic argument:

- No injured victim will lose one penny in compensation from litigation reform. Litigation reform is aimed at reducing fees and shortening the litigation process and makes no change in the law governing compensatory damages.

- Truly deserving victims will still be able to recover their damages through lawsuits after the system is reformed.

- By shortening the litigation process (which fee-shifting aims to do) reform will actually benefit accident victims by helping them recover their damages faster.

- The excessive attorneys' fees that are encouraged by litigation today do nothing to help the victims of torts. By reforming litigation to reduce those attorneys' fees, reform takes nothing away from victims.

- Compensatory damages give back to a tort victim everything that was lost through its injury; punitive damages are in excess of those amounts. Limiting punitive damages takes nothing away from the fair compensation owed to a victim.

While the public relations efforts surrounding litigation reform will never be easy, emphasizing the personal impacts of economic effects and the way that injured parties will continue to be able to obtain compensation is the only way to tell this story. That the story can be told is evident from the experiences of Ohio, California, Mississippi and Texas. The process of reform has a long way to go, but it appears to be gaining momentum.

Afterword

After I completed the text of this book in the first few days of January 2005, the Georgia General Assembly began its 2005 session. Among the bills introduced was Senate Bill 3, which included a number of reforms aimed primarily at reducing medical malpractice litigation (including limits on noneconomic damages) but which also included an offer of judgment provision that would have applied to all civil litigation in the state.[179] As originally introduced, the offer of judgment rule in Georgia's S.B. 3 is substantially the same as the offer of judgment rule in Florida. The rule in S.B. 3 allows either the plaintiff or the defendant to make an offer of judgment and shifts reasonable costs and attorneys' fees if the offer is declined and the resulting judgment is at least 25% less favorable than the amount of the offer.

Already the political battle is taking shape. One of the key supporters of the bill, the Medical Association of Georgia ("MAG") has identified a number of medical practices in the state that have closed because of the increase in malpractice liability insurance. MAG is also proposing a limit on noneconomic damages, arguing that compensatory damages make a plaintiff whole and noneconomic damages merely act as a windfall. MAG's spokesperson was quoted to say, "The tort system is designed to make a plaintiff whole…It's not designed to make them rich."[180] Opponents of the measure, including the American Association of Retired Persons and some consumer watchdog groups were quick to accuse the measure of putting patient safety at risk. Opponents had assembled a handful of medical malpractice victims to make their case more sympathetic. One person, the mother of a young child who was supposedly blinded through a medical error, was quoted to criticize the cap on damages by saying, "If you lost your eyesight because of a doctor would you be satisfied with $250,000?"[181]

---

179. Georgia Senate Bill 3 *available at* http://www.legis.state.ga. us/legis/2005_06/fulltext/sb3.htm.

180. Bill Rankin, *Legislature to Try Again on Tort Reform*, ATLANTA JOURNAL CONSTITUTION (Metro p. 1) (Jan. 2, 2005) *available at* http://www.ajc.com/news/content/ metro/1204/02tort.html.

181. *Id.*

It is too early to tell what will become of this bill but it presages hope for reform to see states continuing to look to fee-shifting measures as tools to reform the litigation system. As it was in Mississippi in 2003 and 2004, the Republican party won control of both houses of the Georgia legislature in the 2004 general election for the first time since Reconstruction. Together with a Republican governor, this shift in control of the state government signals the potential for systemic change in Georgia's litigation laws. The incoming Speaker of the Georgia House, Glenn Richardson, a lawyer who has represented plaintiffs in medical malpractice cases, and who seems ideally situated to make the case for reform, has said that reform is important to the people of his state and to his agenda.

APPENDIX A

States with Limitations on Punitive Damages

(See Chapter 6 for a description of these abbreviations)

State	Any Limit	Ratio Limit	Std of Proof	Citation/Notes
Alabama	X	3x, variable	X	
Alaska	X	3x, variable	X	Code Section 9-17-020.
Arizona	X			Applies only to drug-related claims
Arkansas	X	3x, variable	X	Code Section 16-55-206—207 (providing the standards for awarding punitive damages) and Code Section 16-55-208 (limiting punitive damages to three times compensatory damages, subject to other limitations).
California	X		X	
Colorado	X	1x		
Connecticut				
Delaware				
District of Columbia				

State	Any Limit	Ratio Limit	Std of Proof	Citation/Notes
Florida	X	3x—4x, variable	X	Limitations on punitive damages do not apply to cases involving the abuse of the elderly, children, or drunk driving. Fla. Stat. 768.73 F
Georgia	X	$250,000 flat	X	O.C.G.A. 51-12-5.1 requires a separate proceeding to award punitive damages, requires "clear and convincing" evidence and caps all awards at $250,000.
Hawaii				
Idaho	X	3x, variable	X	Code Sec. 6-1604.
Illinois	Φ			
Indiana	X	3x, variable		Requires 75% of punitive damages award to be paid to a state fund. Indiana Code 34-51-3.
Iowa	X		X	Requires 75% of punitive damages award to be paid to a state fund. Code Sec. 668A.1
Kansas	X	Up to $5 million, based on defendant's income	X	Code Sec. 60-3701.
Kentucky	Φ			
Louisiana	X			Special statute involving handling of hazardous substances.
Maine				
Maryland				
Massachusetts				
Michigan				

State	Any Limit	Ratio Limit	Std of Proof	Citation/Notes
Minnesota	X			Requires showing of "deliberate disregard." Requires separate proceeding for consideration of punitive damages. Award of punitive damages can be reviewed by appellate courts. Minn. Stat. Sec 549.20
Mississippi	X	Based on defendant's net worth	X	Also prohibits punitive damages unless there are compensatory damages.
Missouri	X			Requires separate proceeding for consideration of punitive damages. Requires 50% of punitive damages to be paid to state fund. Code Sec. 537.675.
Montana	X	Variable	X	Punitive damages limited to lesser of $10 million or 3 percent of defendant's net worth. No limitation on punitive damages awards in class actions. Code Sec. 27-1-220.
Nebraska				
Nevada	X	Variable	X	Punitive damages may not exceed $300,000 where the compensatory damages are less than $100,000 and may not exceed 3 times the compensatory damages when the compensatory damages are $100,000 or more. Nev. Rev. Stat. 42.005. Caps do not apply in cases for products liability, insurer bad faith, housing discrimination, defamation and certain environmental claims.
New Hampshire	X	Flat		Prohibits all punitive damages. Code Sec. 506:16. Non-economic damages are limited to $875,000. Code Sec. 508:4-d.

State	Any Limit	Ratio Limit	Std of Proof	Citation/Notes
New Jersey	X	Greater of 5 times compensatory damages or $350,000.		Limitation does not apply to bias crimes, discrimination, disclosure of AIDS test results, sexual abuse or damages caused by drunk driving. Requires a separate proceeding for punitive damages awards. Code Sec. 2A:15-5.
New Mexico				
New York	X			Requires than 20% of punitive damages awards be paid to state fund.
North Carolina	X	3x, variable	X	Requires separate proceeding for punitive damages.
North Dakota	X	2x, variable	X	N.D. Cent. Code § 32003.2-11(4).
Ohio	Φ			
Oklahoma	X	Variable, from 1x to 2x	X	Okla. Stat., Tit. 23, §§ 9.1(B)-(D)
Oregon	X		X	Requires 60% of punitive damages be paid to state fund. Prohibits payment of more than 20% of punitive damages award to prevailing attorney. Code Sec. 31.730, 735.
Pennsylvania				
Rhode Island				
South Carolina	X		X	
South Dakota	X		X	
Tennessee				
Texas	X	2x, variable	X	Requires unanimous jury verdict to award punitive damages.

State	Any Limit	Ratio Limit	Std of Proof	Citation/Notes
Utah	X		X	Requires separate proceeding for punitive damages. Requires 50% of all punitive damages awards over $20,000 be paid to state fund.
Vermont				
Virginia	X	$350,000 flat		Va. Code Ann. §8.01-38.1
Washington				
West Virginia				
Wisconsin	X			Requires showing that defendant acted "maliciously or in intentional disregard of the rights of the plain-tiff."
Wyoming				
TOTAL	34*	19	20	

*   Of the 34 states adopting some kind of limitation on punitive damages, the limitation was ruled unconstitutional in 3 of those states.

X—Indicates some kind of limitation on punitive damages
Φ—Indicates some kind of limitation was adopted but was declared unconstitutional and no further kind of limitation was adopted.
Adapted from Tort Reform Record, American Tort Reform Association (July 13, 2004 edition) *available at* http:// www.atra.org/.

Appendix B

Model Statute to Limit Punitive Damages

Section 1   In any civil action in this state in which punitive damages are permitted, no party may recover punitive damages in an amount that exceeds the following limitations:

a.   an amount that is equal to one times the amount of compensatory damages awarded to the party in the action, unless the requirements of subsection (b) are satisfied; or

b.   in a case in which the finder of fact has found the tortfeasor's conduct to be especially reprehensible, in light of whether the harm done to the victim was physical, whether the tortfeasor was indifferent to or recklessly disregarded the health or safety of others, whether the tortfeasor's conduct was intentionally directed towards the financial vulnerability of the victim, whether the tortfeasor's tortious conduct was repeated, and whether the tortfeasor caused harm as a result of intentional malice, trickery or deceit, an amount that is equal to nine times the amount of compensatory damages awarded to the party in the action.

APPENDIX C

Model Statute for Offer of Judgment

Section 1   At any time more than 10 days before the trial of a civil action in the courts of this state, a party defending against a claim may serve upon the adverse party an offer to allow judgment to be taken against the defending party for the money or property or to the effect specified in the offer. If within 10 days after the service of the offer the adverse party serves written notice that the offer is accepted, either party may then file the offer and notice of acceptance together with proof of service thereof and thereupon the clerk shall enter judgment. An offer not accepted shall be deemed withdrawn and evidence thereof is not admissible except in a proceeding to determine costs and attorneys fees. If the judgment finally obtained by the offeree on the claim is not more favorable than the offer on that claim, the offeree must pay the costs and reasonable attorneys fees incurred on that claim after the making of the offer. The fact that an offer is made but not accepted does not preclude a subsequent offer. When the liability of one party to another has been determined by verdict or order or judgment, but the amount or extent of the liability remains to be determined by further proceedings, the party adjudged liable may make an offer of judgment, which shall have the same effect as an offer made before trial if it is served within a reasonable time not less than 10 days prior to the commencement of hearings to determine the amount or extent of liability.

Section 2   For the purpose of determining the reasonable attorneys fees of an offeror and calculating the amount that the offeree must pay as described in Section 1, the court may consider the hourly rates actually charged by the offeror's attorneys, the efforts undertaken by the offeror's attorneys, the quality of the work performed by the offeror's attorneys, the results achieved by the offeror's attorneys, and amounts charged by other lawyers for work similar to that done by the offeror's attorneys; provided, however, that the court may not determine the offeror's reasonable attorneys fees to be less than the amount actually paid by the offeror to the offeror's attorneys in cash.

Bibliography

American Tort Reform Association, *Bringing Justice to Judicial Hellholes* (2003).

P.S. Atiyah, *Tort Law and the Alternatives: Some Anglo-American Comparisons*, 1987 DUKE L.J. 1002, 1012.

David E. Bernstein, *Procedural Tort Reform: Lessons from Other Nations*, REGULATION, Vol. 19 (1996).

Patricia M. Danzon, Andrew J. Epstein, Scott Johnson, *The Crisis in Medical Malpractice Insurance* (The Wharton School, University of Pennsylvania, 2003), *available at* http://fic.wharton.upenn.edu/fic/papers/04/Danzon%20%20Paper.pdf.

Lorraine Wright Feuerstein, *Two-Way Fee Shifting on Summary Judgment or Dismissal: An Equitable Deterrent to Unmeritorious Lawsuits*, 23 PEPP. L. REV. 125 (1995).

Mitu Gulati, Jeffrey J. Rachlinski, Donald C. Langevoort, *Fraud by Hindsight*, (Georgetown Law School, 2002) *available at* http://www.law.georgetown.edu/faculty/documents/gulati.pdf.

Philip Howard, THE COLLAPSE OF THE COMMON GOOD: HOW AMERICA'S LAWSUIT CULTURE UNDERMINES OUR FREEDOM (Ballantine Books 2002)

Mark A. Klugheit, *Where the Rubber Meets the Road: Theoretical Justifications vs. Practical Outcomes in Punitive Damages Litigation*, 52 SYRACUSE L. REV. 803 (2002)

Kevin M. Kordziel, *Note, Rule 82 Revisited: Attorney Fee Shifting in Alaska*, 10 ALASKA L. REV. 429 at 437 (1993).

Herbert M. Kritzer, *Lawyer Fees and Lawyer Behavior in Litigation: What Does the Empirical Literature Really Say?*, 80 TEX. L. REV. 1943 (2002)

Deborah R. Hensler, Thomas D. Rowe, Jr., *Beyond "It Just Ain't Worth It": Alternative Strategies for Damage Class Action Reform*, 64 LAW & CONTEMP. PROBS. 137 (Spring/Summer 2001)

Deborah R. Hensler et al., *Class Action Dilemmas: Pursuing Public Goals for Private Gain* (Executive Summary) (Rand Institute for Civil Justice) (1999) 9-10.

Joni Hersch & W. Kip Viscusi, *Punitive Damages: How Judges and Juries Perform*, 33 J. LEGAL STUD. 1 (2004).

Peter W. Huber, GALILEO'S REVENGE: JUNK SCIENCE IN THE COURTROOM (1991)

Peter W. Huber, LIABILITY: THE LEGAL REVOLUTION AND ITS CONSEQUENCES (Basic Books 1988)

J. Clark Kelso and Kari C. Kelso, *An Analysis of Punitive Damages in California Courts, 1991-2000* (2001) *available at* http://www.cjac.org.

Walter Olson and David Bernstein, *Loser-Pays: Where Next?*, 55 MD. L. REV. 1161 (1996).

Walter Olson, THE RULE OF LAWYERS (Truman Talley Books 2004).

Charlie Ross, *Winning the Tort War in Mississippi* (American Tort Reform Association, 2004) *available at* http://www.atra.org.

W. Kip Viscusi, *The Regulation-Litigation Interaction,* (American Enterprise Institute—Brookings Joint Center, 2001) *available at* http://www.aei.brookings.org/admin/authorpdfs/page.php?id=159.

W. Kip Viscusi, et al., REGULATION THROUGH LITIGATION, (American Enterprise Institute—Brookings Joint Center, 2002).

W. Kip. Viscusi, *Why There is No Defense of Punitive Damages*, 87 GEO. L.J. 381, 392 (1998).

W. Kip Viscusi, *Punitive Damages: How Jurors Fail to Promote Efficiency*, 39 HARV. J. OF LEGIS. 139 (2002).

Panel Discussion, *The New Class Action Targets: Are Class Actions Undermining Regulation in the Fields of Financial Services, High Technology and Telecommunications?* (Center for Legal Policy at the Manhattan Institute, October 30, 2002) *available at* http://www.fed-soc.org/Publications/Transcripts/classactions1.pdf.

Glossary

Action—a proceeding in court to enforce the rights of a party; *see also* Cause of Action.

Bench Trial—a trial conducted by a judge without a jury.

Cause of Action—A legal right that is capable of being enforced in a lawsuit. Generally speaking, causes of action may arise from torts or from contracts.

Civil Action—a lawsuit between two or more parties for the purpose of vindicating private causes of action. *Compare* to Criminal Action.

Common Law—the body of judge-made law recognized in most courts, deriving its authority from historical precedent and the decisions of prior courts rather than from statute or the actions of the legislature.

Compensatory Damages—that portion of a plaintiff's damages that consists of the amount of money required to put the plaintiff back into the position plaintiff would have been if not for the wrongdoing of the defendant. *See also* Damages.

Complaint—the initial filing that begins a lawsuit by summarizing the causes of action the plaintiff is claiming against the defendant.

Contract—a legally enforceable agreement among two or more parties.

Criminal Action—an action by the government to enforce the criminal law against individuals. *Compare* to Civil Action.

Damages—the measure of harm done to an injured party for which the injured party may have a cause of action. *See also* Compensatory Damages, Economic Damages, Noneconomic Damages and Punitive Damages.

Defendant—the party who is sued in a lawsuit.

Discovery—the stage of a civil action in which the parties can use the compulsory power of the court to collect documents from each other and from third parties, compel individuals to submit to depositions, answer interrogatories and produce documents and other potential evidence.

Economic Damages—that portion of a plaintiff's damages that consist of plaintiff's economic losses, such as medical expenses, lost wages and loss of earning potential.

Federal Rules—the Federal Rules of Civil Procedure (abbreviated as Fed. R. Civ. P.); the body of rules enacted by Congress to govern the conduct of lawsuits in federal courts.

Judgment—an order of a court in favor of a party that disposes of a cause of action, either dismissing the action or granting relief to the party who is prosecuting the action.

Noneconomic Damages—that portion of a plaintiff's damages that consist of harms suffered by the plaintiff that have no extrinsic economic value, such as damages from pain, suffering and mental anguish.

Plaintiff—the party who initiates a lawsuit.

Plaintiffs' Attorney—an attorney who primarily performs services on behalf of plaintiffs.

Preliminary Motion—a motion that seeks to dispose of a cause of action at an early stage in the proceedings, usually before the summary judgment stage. A defendant who seeks to dispose of a complaint on a preliminary motion, generally speaking, must demonstrate that even if all of the plaintiff's allegations were true the plaintiff would still not be entitled to judgment.

Punitive Damages—a form of relief that a plaintiff can seek for certain kinds of intentional damages; an award of punitive damages is generally considered to represent society's interest in retribution and in deterring similar wrongful conduct in the future. *See also* Damages.

Relief—the money or other court action sought by a party who is prosecuting a cause of action.

Summary Judgment—an order issued by a court that dismisses a case prior to trial by finding that, taking all of the evidence in the light most favorable to the party that opposes summary judgment, there is no genuine issue of material fact and the party seeking judgment is entitled to judgment as a matter of law.

Tort—an actionable civil wrong; a cause of action that exists under common law; negligence, trespass, slander, libel, assault and conversion are examples of kinds of torts.

Trial—the stage of a civil action in which the parties present evidence, whether to the court or to a jury.

Index

978-0-595-34717-9
0-595-34717-7